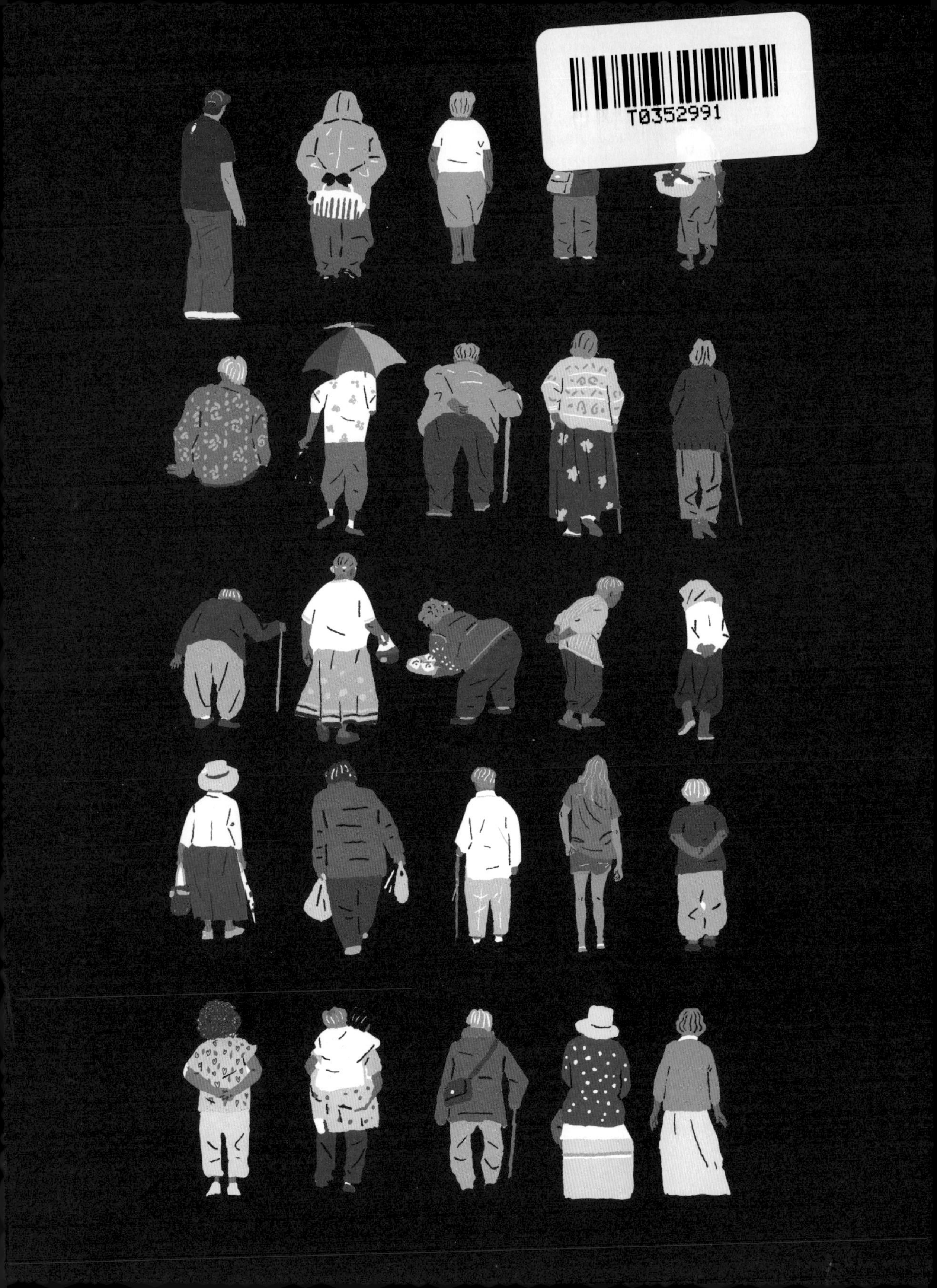

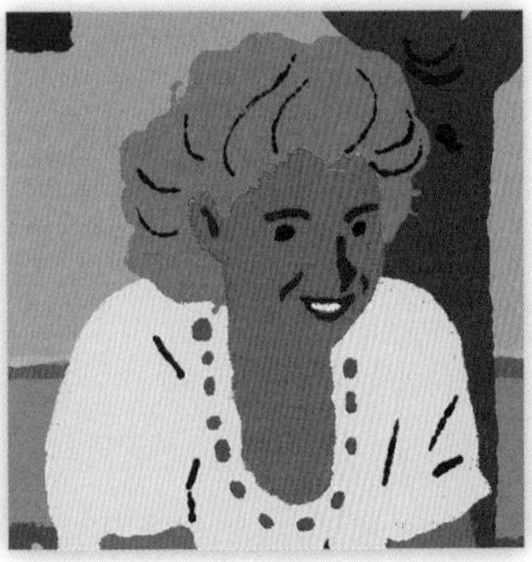
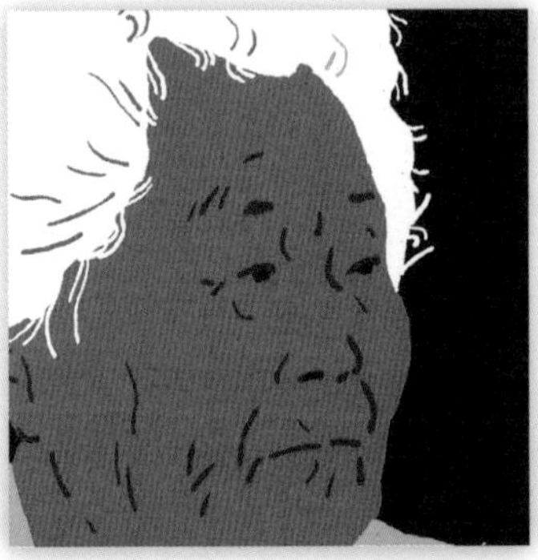
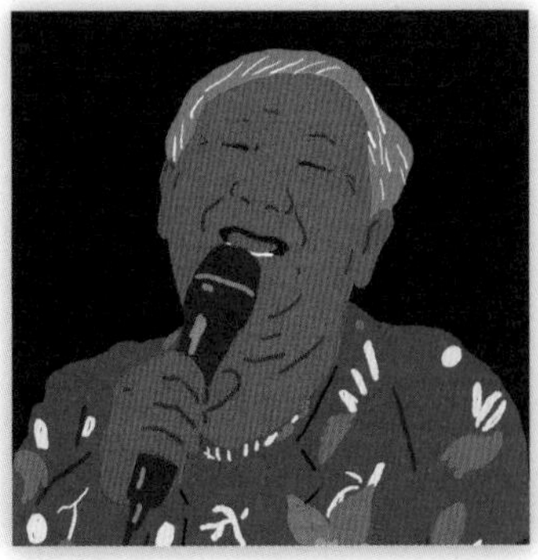
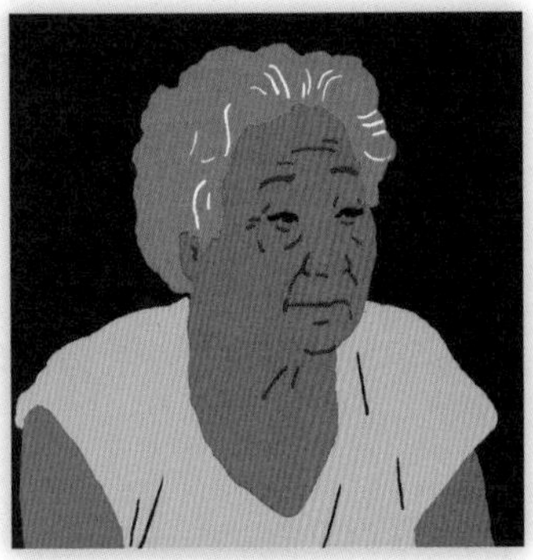
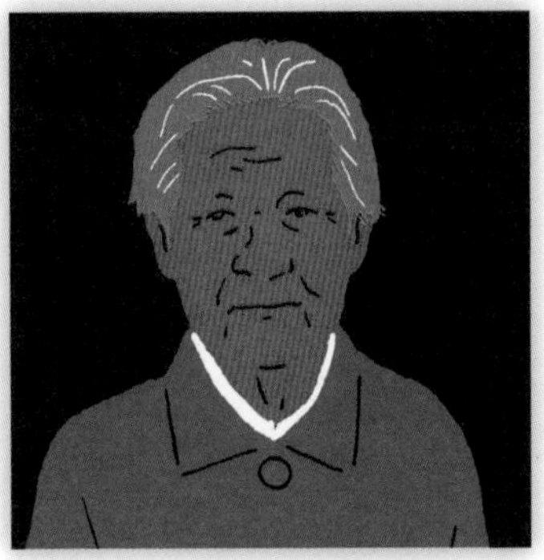
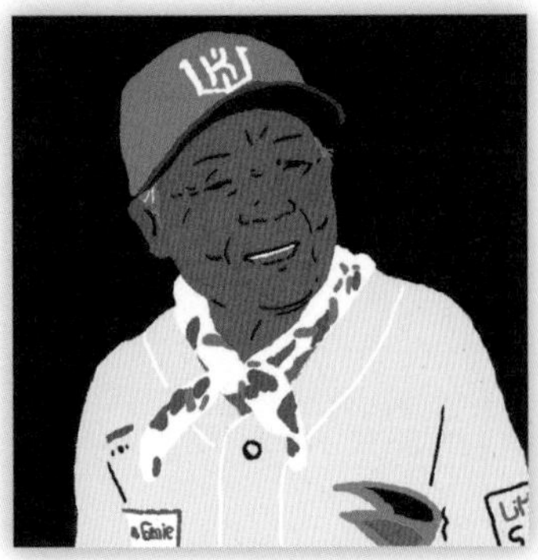
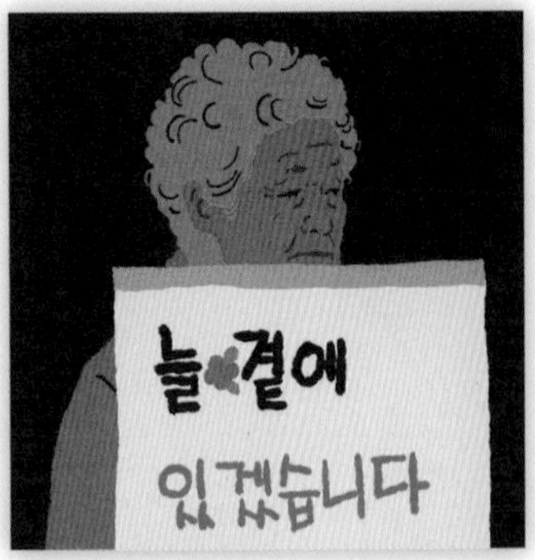
늘 곁에
있겠습니다
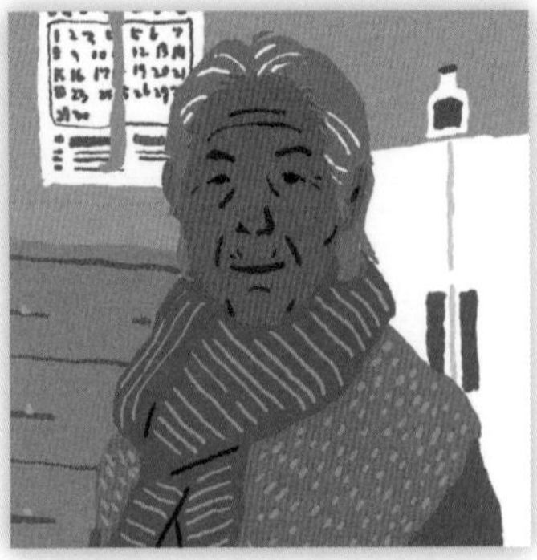
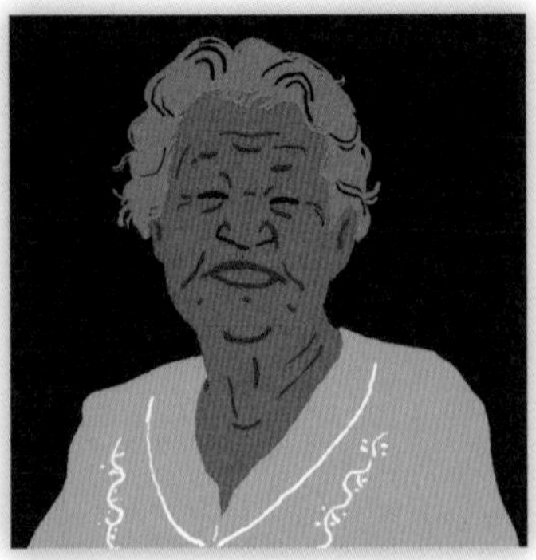
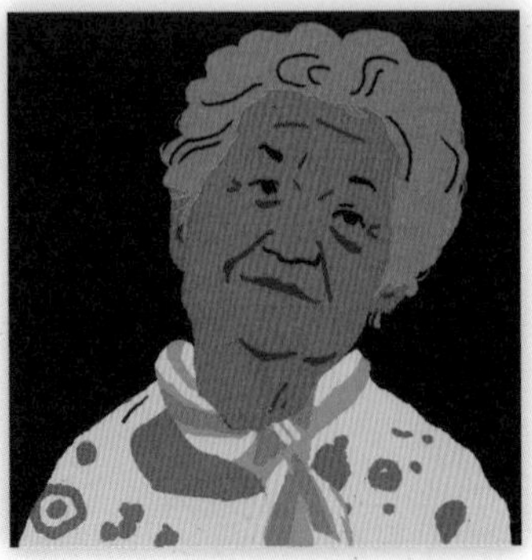
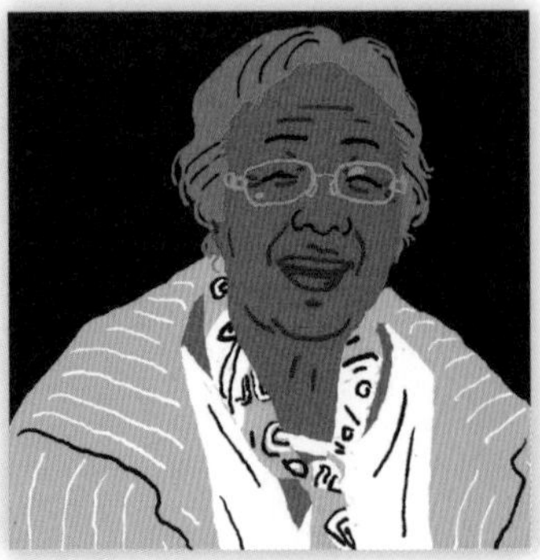
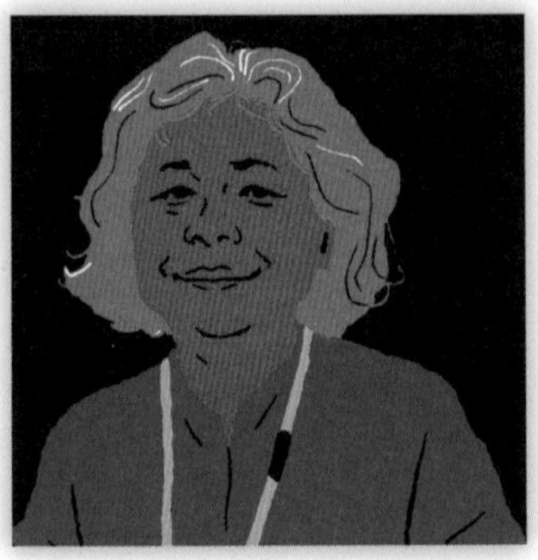

Grandmothers, Our Grandmothers

Remembering the "Comfort Women" of World War II

Han Seong-won

TUTTLE Publishing

Tokyo | Rutland, Vermont | Singapore

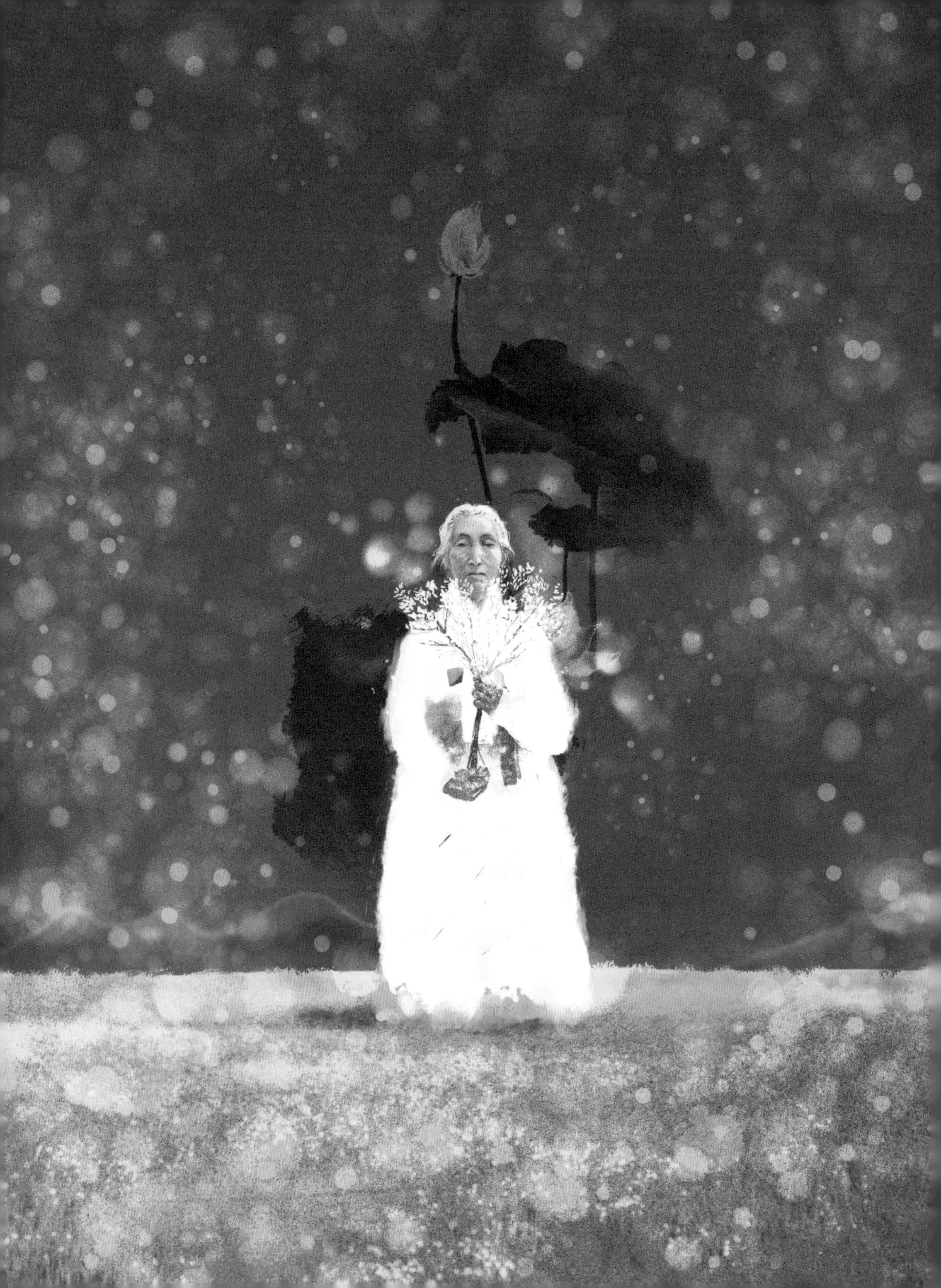

Contents

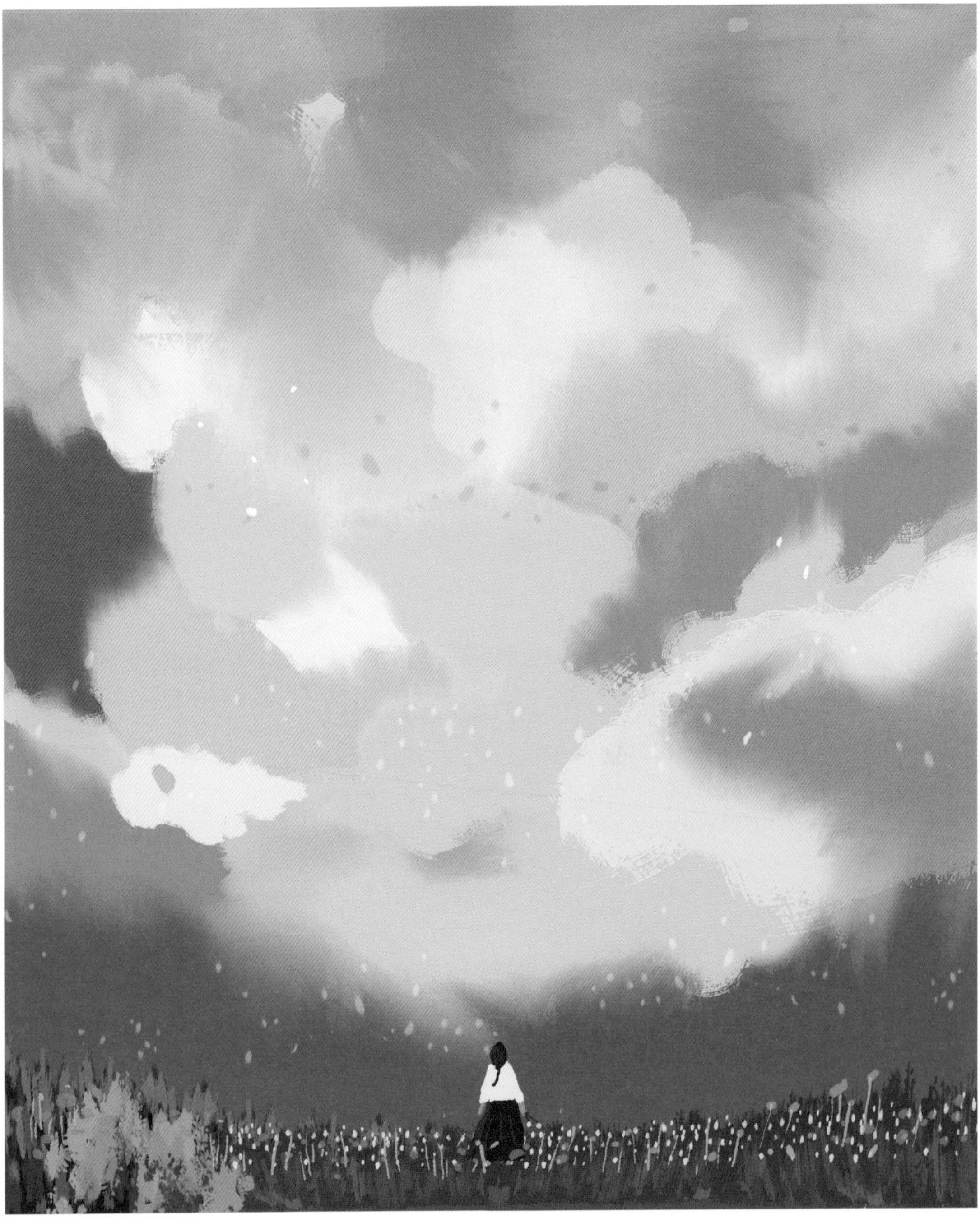

From the Stance of Bystander to That of a Keeper of Records

The harrowing memories of war leave indelible wounds on victims. War does not end on the battlefields. Victims live with lasting wounds and trauma. Even if they receive an exact and sincere apology from the perpetrators, much time must pass before the injuries inflicted on the victims are healed. However, the Grandmothers who suffered as "comfort women" for the Japanese Imperial Army have received no such apology, even to this day. Their wounds remain unhealed.

Twenty years ago, I started making drawings on the subject of modern Korean history and, as if fate had led me to it, I ended up periodically drawing about this part of Korea's story. I worked on an illustration project, "War and Women," for a KBS (Korea Broadcast Station) documentary and wrote about people who experienced war first-hand while working on recording the Jeam-ri: Site of where massacre by the Japanese Imperial Army against independence protesters took place from March 1st, 1919.

After a series of delays for various reasons, in February 2019 I started recording the painful history of war's aftermath and drawing related images. I felt this work was the current-day artist's responsibility and that it is a personal duty, like unfinished homework. I wanted to record in earnest both the lives of those who had experienced war and our own perspectives on their memories of what actually happened.

I drew pictures of the daily lives and stories of Grandmothers who had been the Japanese Imperial Army's "comfort women" and the brave actions of those women who spoke out. I read related books, participated in Wednesday Protests, collected newspaper articles, and visited frequently the War and Women's Rights Museum in order to understand as well as I possibly could the pain of our Grandmothers. As the project unfolded I had opportunities to visit the Grandmothers themselves, these remarkable women who became human rights activists.

Receiving advice and help from activists, participating in protests and sharing the stories of citizens who got together with warm hearts, I contemplated the things that we should remember together and never allow ourselves to forget. My hope is that our actions may provide some small healing to the Grandmothers who have been living with such painful and horrible memories.

Recording the stories of the Grandmothers required caution and discretion. I came to understand the need for recovery from the violation of basic rights, as well as the restoration of those rights, and how this must be approached with sensitivity in our activism, for the sake of these Grandmothers, and for all of humanity as we strive for peace.

My wish is that readers will take inspiration from the stories of these Grandmothers. My drawings depict the ordinary but beautiful lives of these courageous Grandmothers rather than images of their sufferings. Through these drawings, I hope we can close the physical, temporal, and emotional distance between the Grandmothers and us. I believe a sense of closeness and empathy will narrow that distance. Instead of seeing only the painful past when we look upon the Grandmothers, I hope we can find our neighbors, our families, and even ourselves in them.

—Han Seong-won

CHAPTER 1

Testimony

The Japanese Imperial Army set up "comfort stations"
wherever they created war zones between 1932 to 1945.

When the Pacific War broke out, they lured girls with
false promises of work or forcibly kidnapped them.

But until 1991, the Japanese government
did not acknowledge even once
the existence of "comfort stations" or "comfort women."

The Most Courageous Revelation in the World!

Grandmother Kim Hak-soon

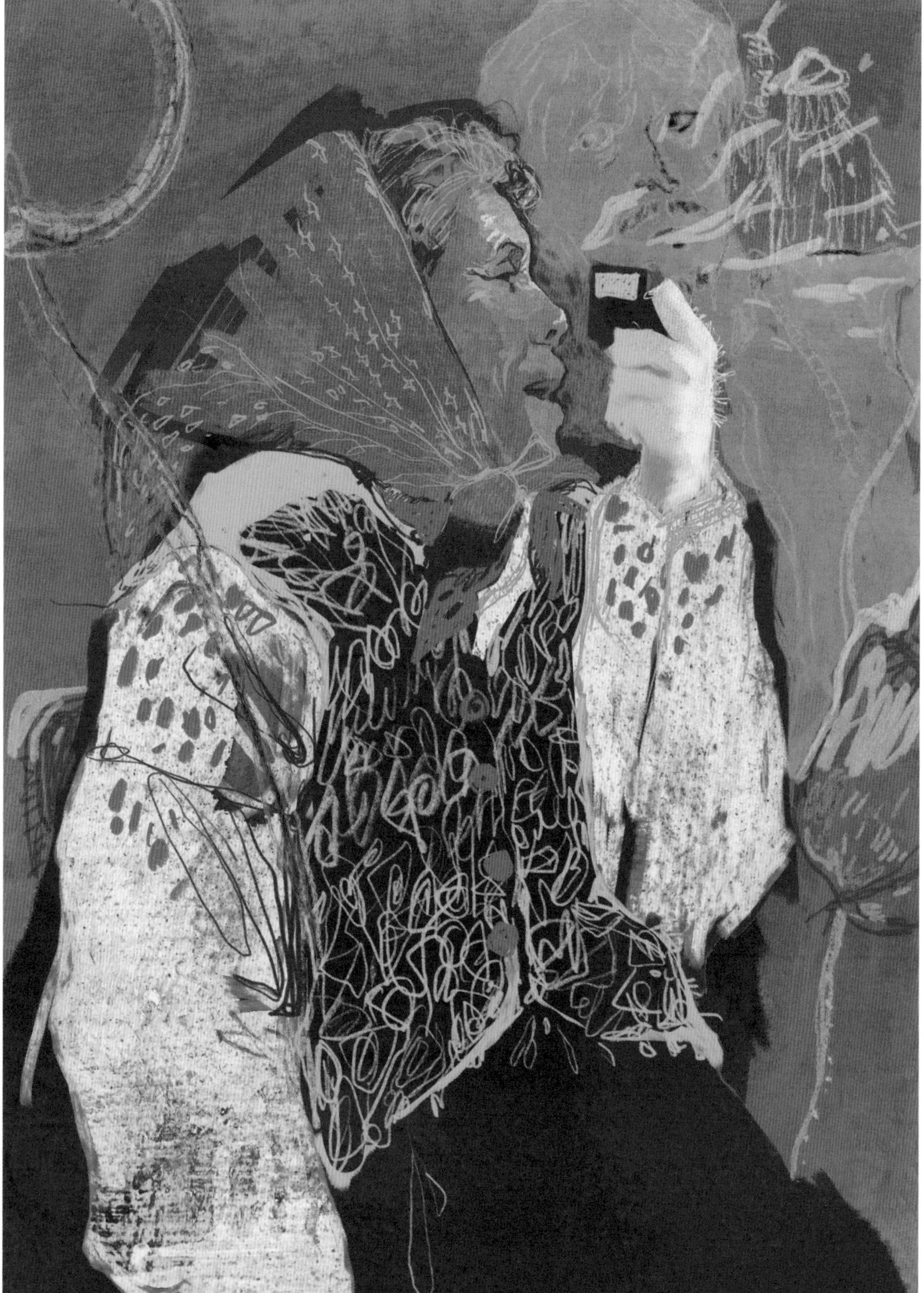

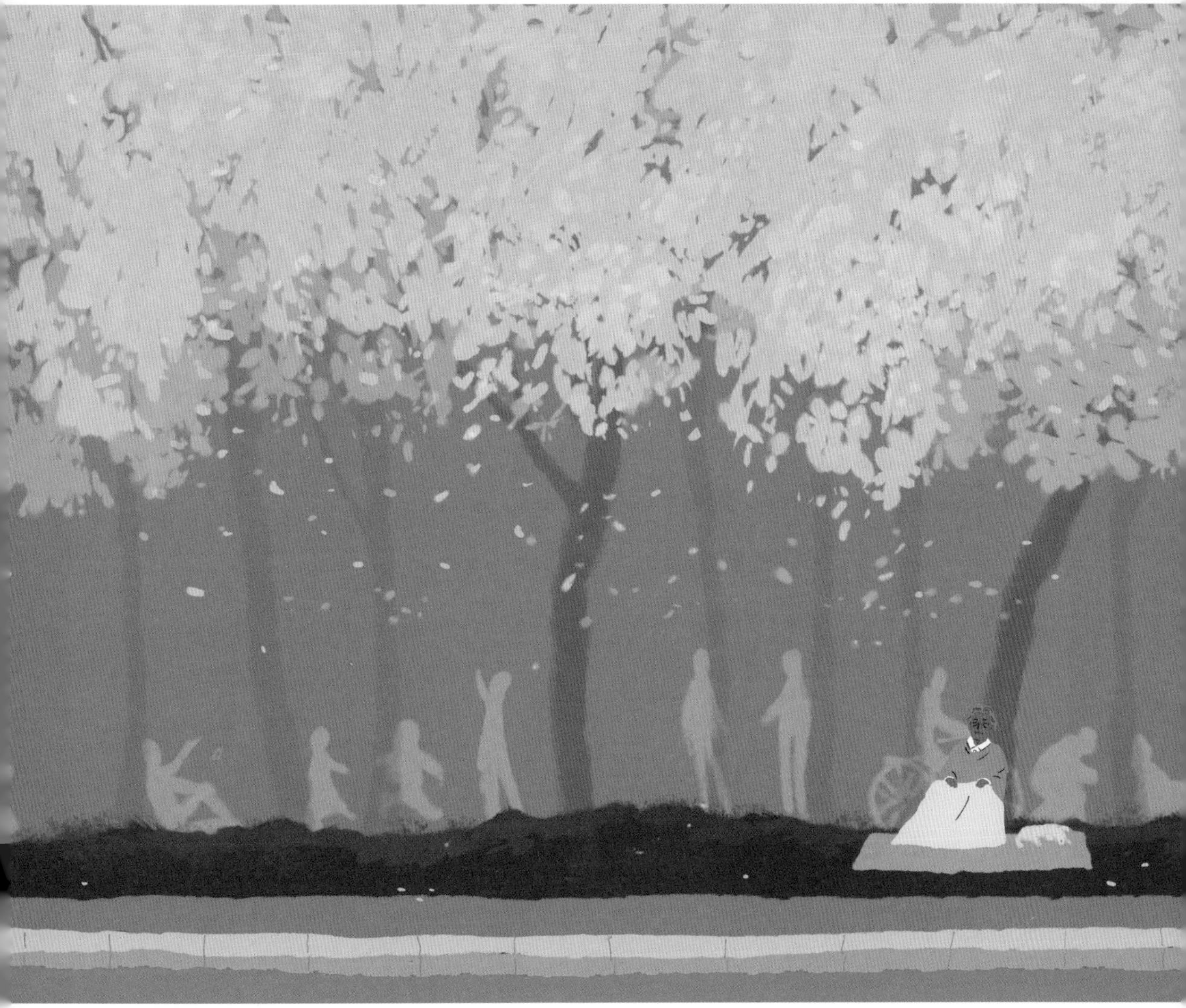

Grandmother Kim Hak-soon was the first to publicly testify on August 14th, 1991 that she was a victim of the Japanese Imperial Army—a"comfort woman"—and filed a lawsuit against the Japanese government.

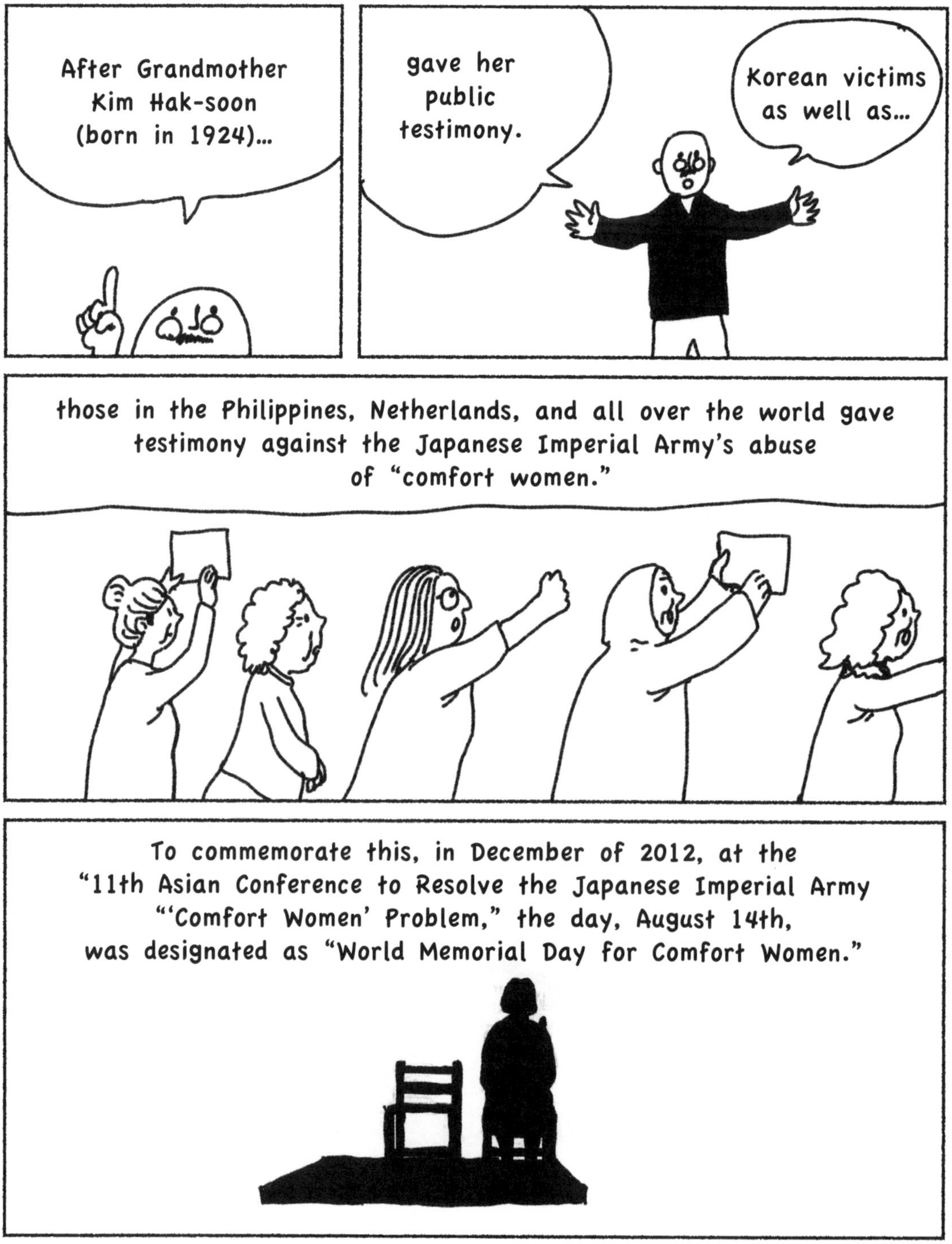
After Grandmother Kim Hak-soon (born in 1924)...
gave her public testimony.
Korean victims as well as...
those in the Philippines, Netherlands, and all over the world gave testimony against the Japanese Imperial Army's abuse of "comfort women."
To commemorate this, in December of 2012, at the "11th Asian Conference to Resolve the Japanese Imperial Army "'Comfort Women' Problem," the day, August 14th, was designated as "World Memorial Day for Comfort Women."

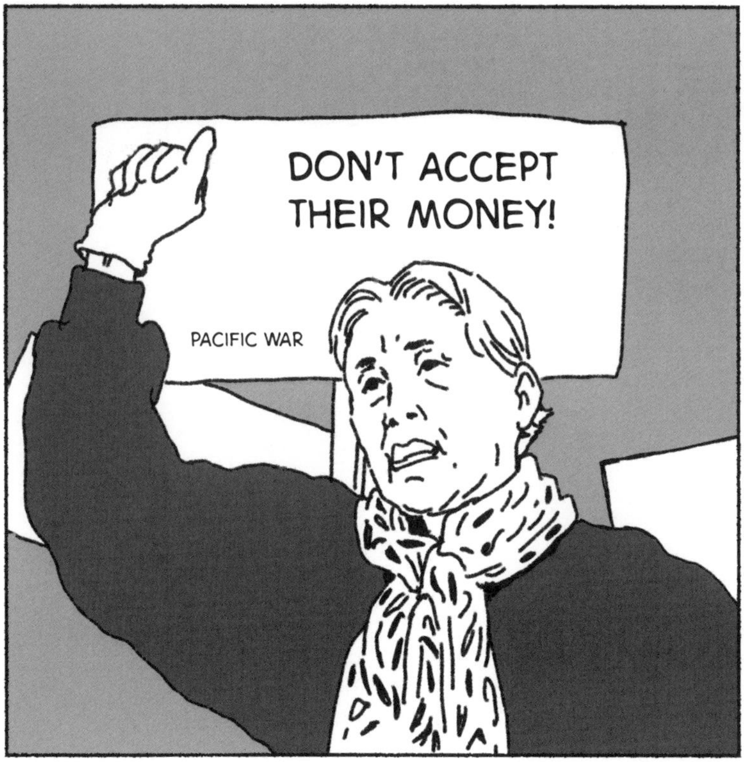
DON'T ACCEPT THEIR MONEY!
PACIFIC WAR

In 2017, the South Korean government also designated August 14th as a memorial day for "comfort women." This day became a national holiday to let the "comfort women" issue be known at home and abroad.

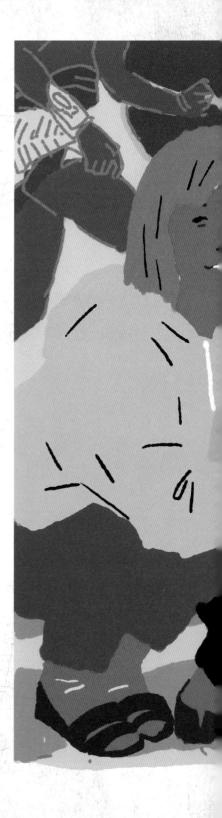

From Peace Activist
to Human Rights Activist

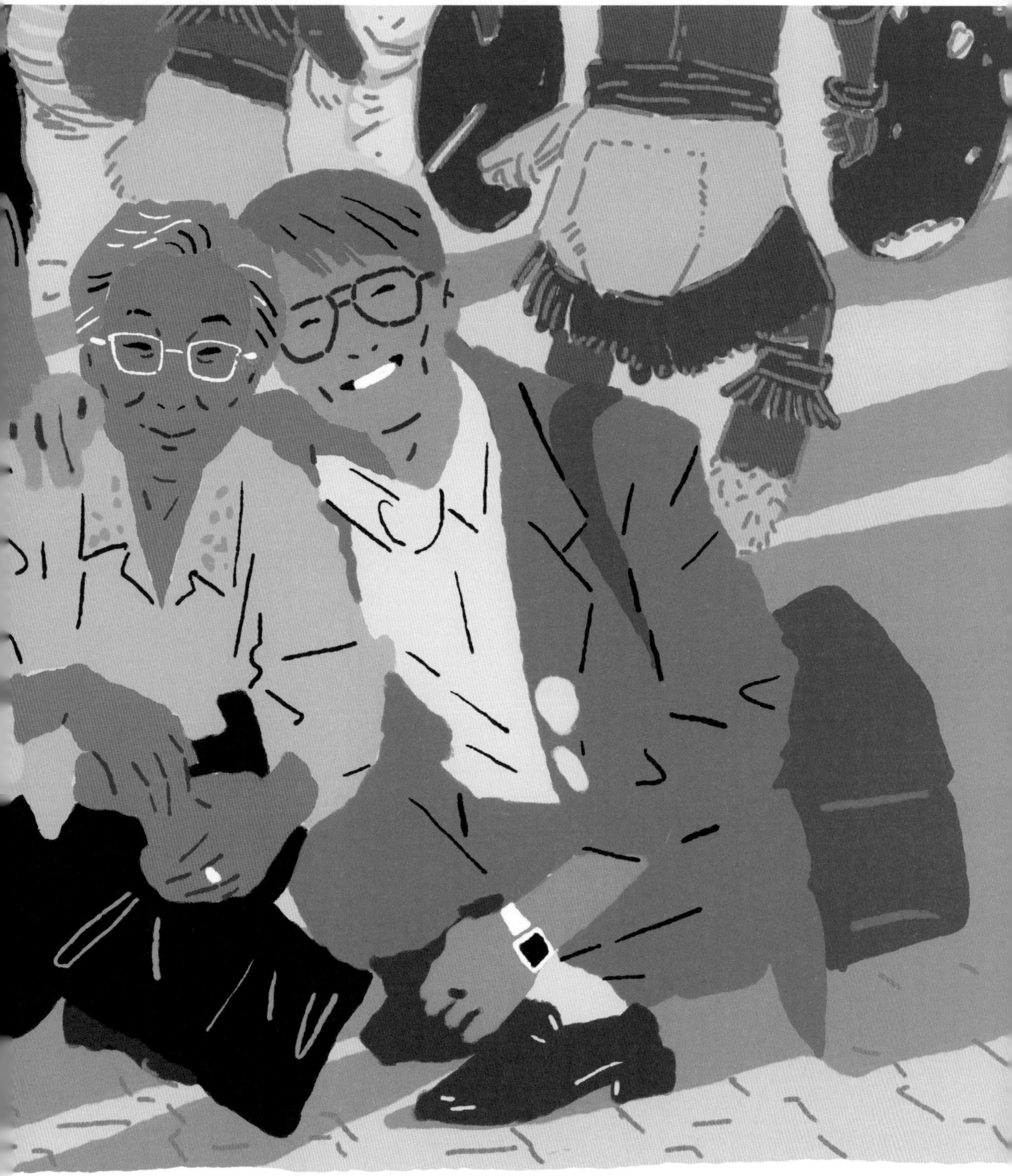

Grandmother Kim Bok-dong

Grandmother Kim Bok-dong was a "comfort woman" who fought for the human rights of women war victims all over the world.

Grandmother Kim Bok-dong had beautifully combed hair and...

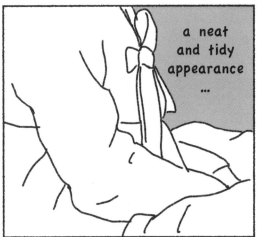

a neat and tidy appearance ...

and a serene smile on her face. She was a lovely Grandmother.

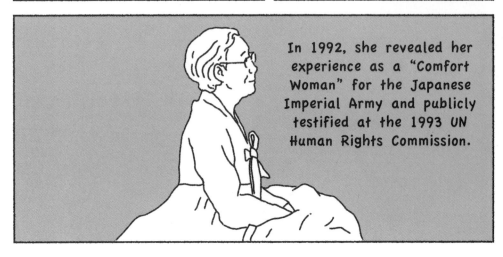

In 1992, she revealed her experience as a "Comfort Woman" for the Japanese Imperial Army and publicly testified at the 1993 UN Human Rights Commission.

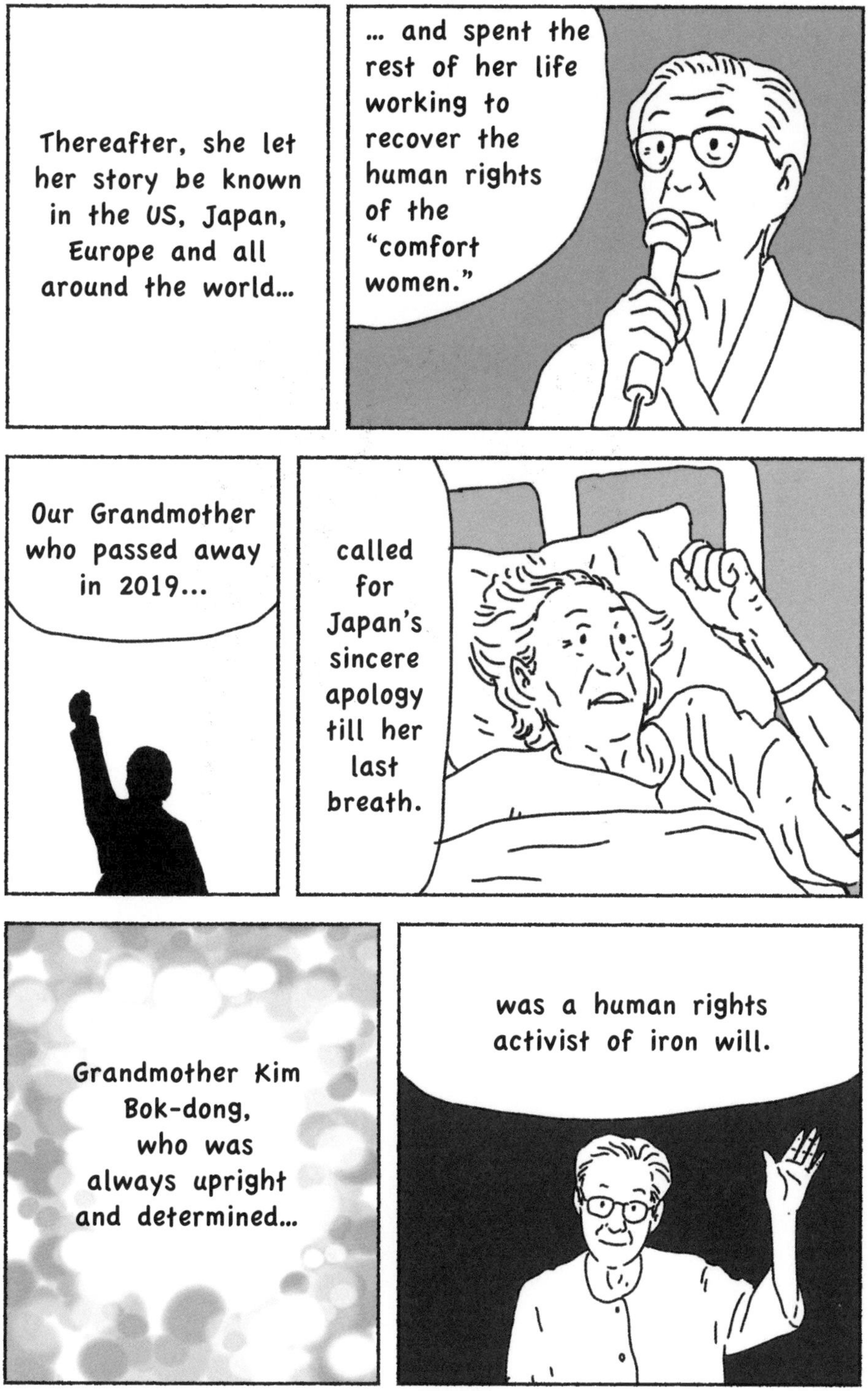
Thereafter, she let her story be known in the US, Japan, Europe and all around the world...
... and spent the rest of her life working to recover the human rights of the "comfort women."
Our Grandmother who passed away in 2019...
called for Japan's sincere apology till her last breath.
Grandmother Kim Bok-dong, who was always upright and determined...
was a human rights activist of iron will.

Sister, Let's Go Home Now!

The beloved youngest daughter
who lived in a house where in the yard
a large persimmon tree grew.

Grandmother Kang Il-chul

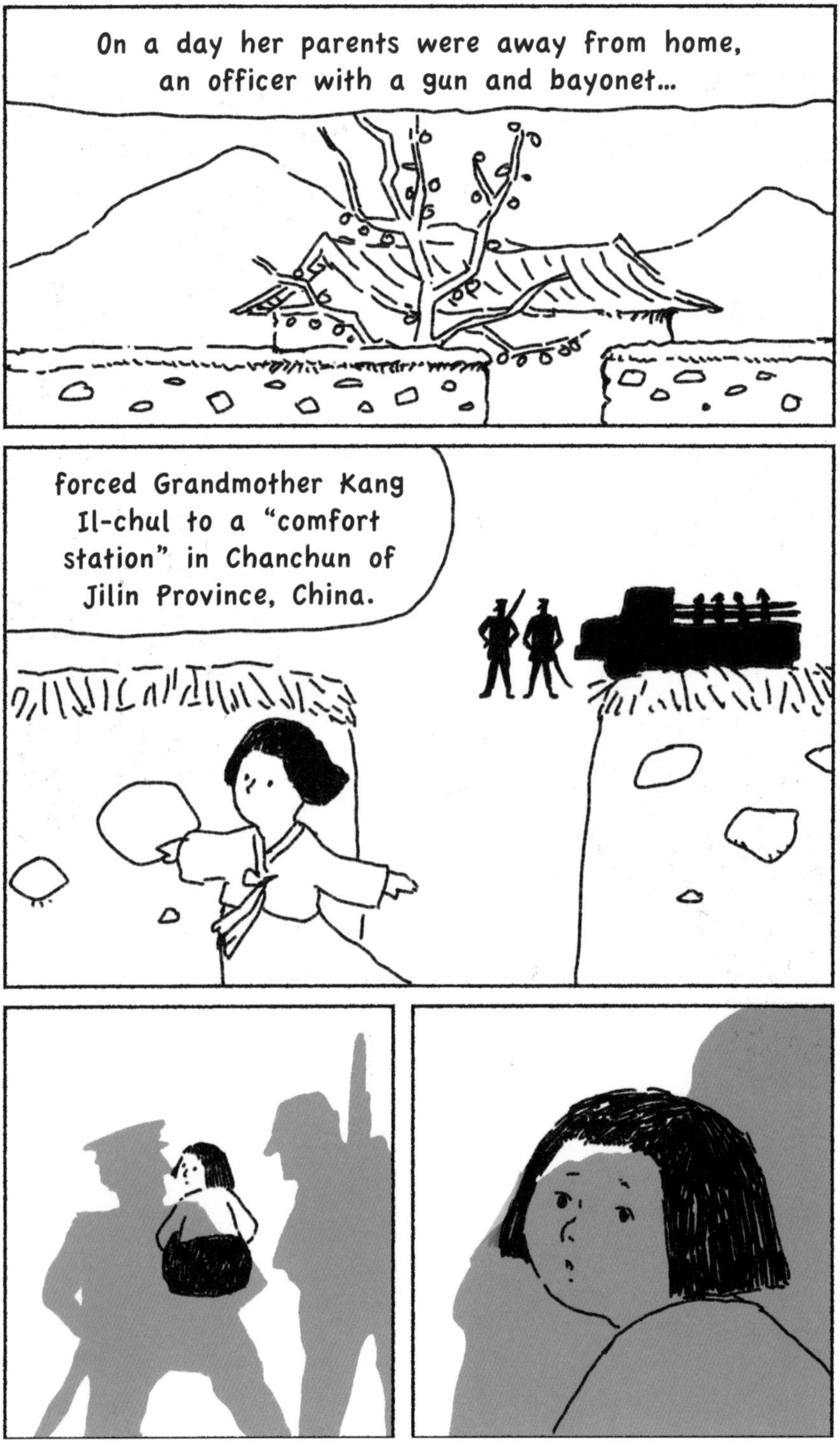
On a day her parents were away from home, an officer with a gun and bayonet...
forced Grandmother Kang Il-chul to a "comfort station" in Chanchun of Jilin Province, China.

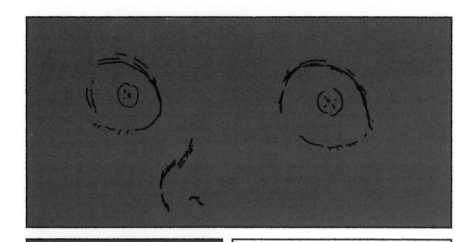

After Grandmother Kang contracted typhoid fever, she was taken outside the "comfort station"...

and the Japanese soldiers tried to burn her alive, but she narrowly escaped.

The 2016 movie, *Spirits' Homecoming*, is based on Grandmother Kang Il-chul's story.

We hope Grandmother Kang Il-Chul who enjoys tending her little vegetable garden, will continue to have many happy days ahead of her.

* 2016 movie based on real stories of "comfort women" by movie director, Cho Jung-rae.

Grandmother Kang Il-chul at the Lincoln Memorial in Washington.

In 2014, Grandmother was invited to the opening ceremony of "The Japanese Army 'Comfort Women' Commemoration Peace Park" in Fairfax, Virginia. While the memories are painful to Grandmother, she has one purpose for her activities and testimonies:

"What hapened to me should never be repeated."

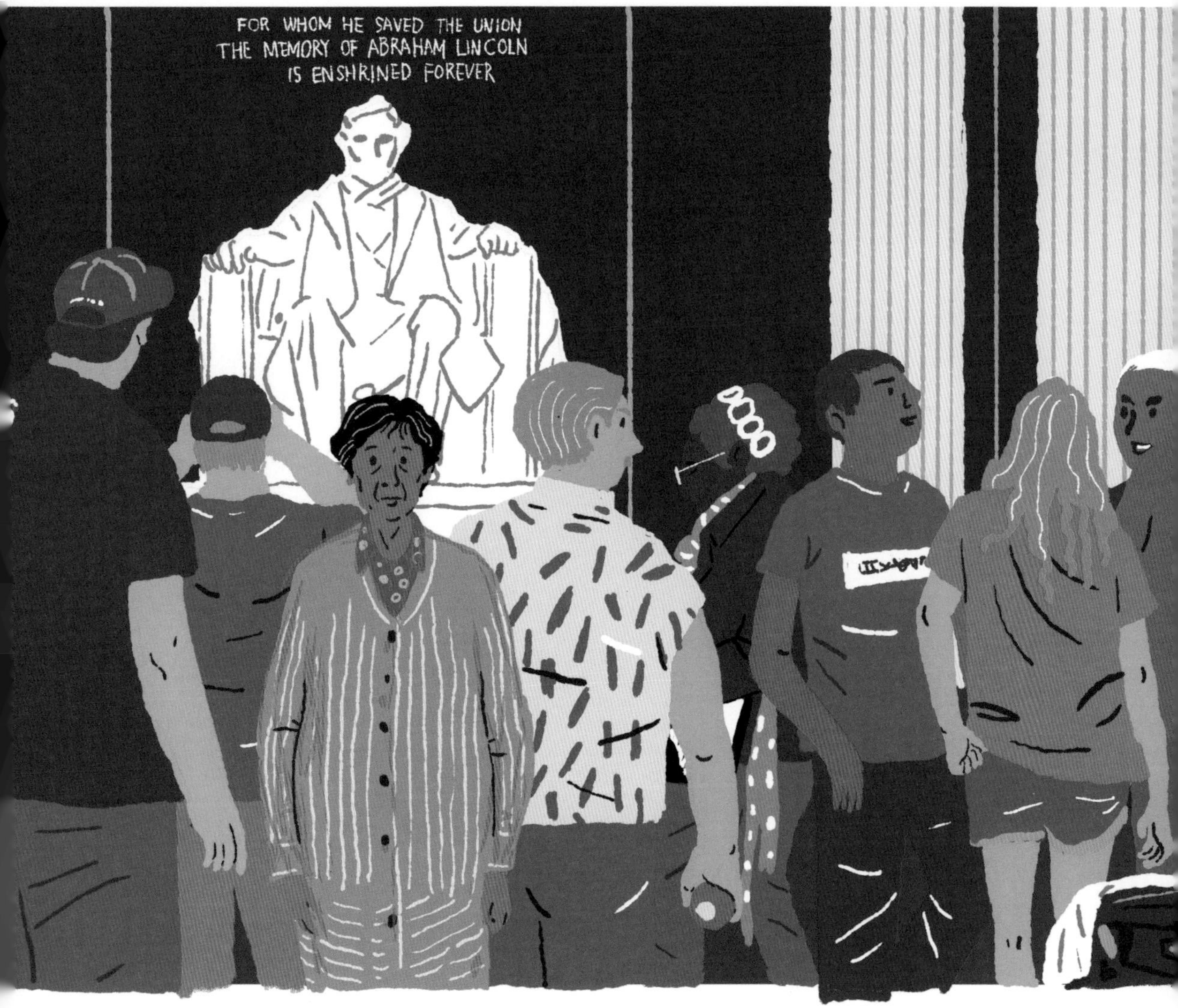
FOR WHOM HE SAVED THE UNION
THE MEMORY OF ABRAHAM LINCOLN
IS ENSHRINED FOREVER

The Names of Girls on the White Handkerchief

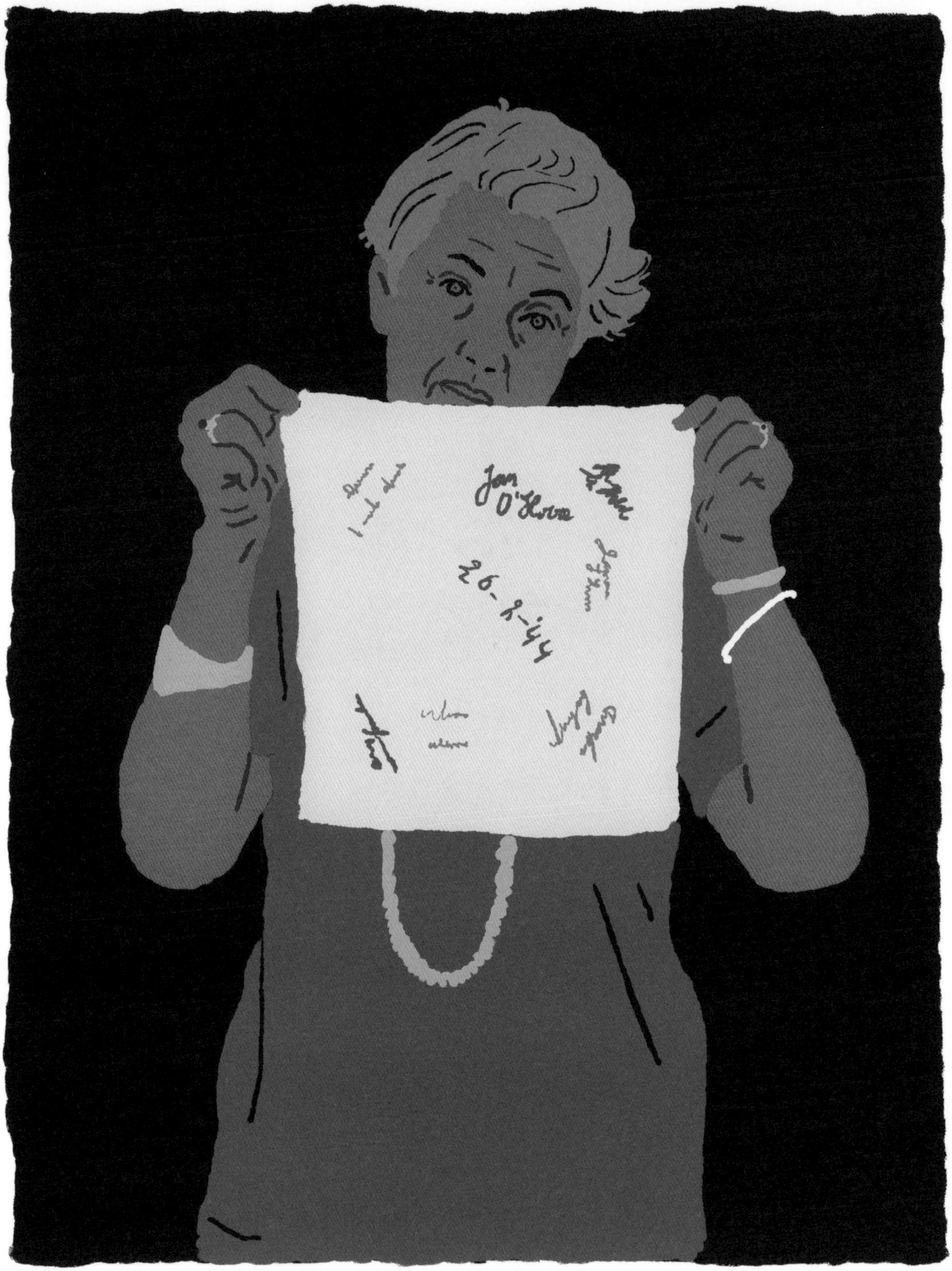
Jan O'Herne
26-2-'44

Grandmother Jan Ruff O'Herne

War ...

Danger to her family

Little space

Rodents

Lack of food

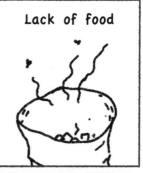

Wretched life in prison camps

But these were all luxuries compared
to the experiences of the 16 girls
who were forced into trucks.

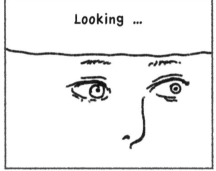

Looking ...

around the room ...

Double bed

Table

Water bottle

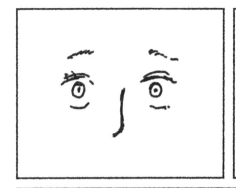

Grandmother lived a nightmare life as a sex slave on Jawa Island in Indonesia. The Japanese Army-run "comfort station" was called Chilhaejung.

Because she was given a Japanese flower name and there was a flower vase in the room...

for 50 years Grandmother could not love flowers.

She and her fellow victims encouraged
each other and prayed daily while enduring hell.

Grandmother kept a white handkerchief and
sewed the names of the girls who arrived there
and their arrival dates.

The handkerchief that she kept with her always
and hidden from her family is now on display at the
Australian War Memorial's World War II exhibition.
It is one of the most important records of war.

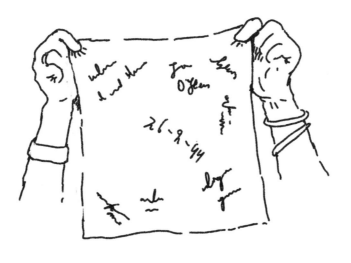

Grandmother Jan Ruff O'Herne is
an Australian from the Netherlands.
She was the first non-Asian to testify
about the horrors of sexual slavery
by the Japanese Imperial Army.

She was inspired to break her silence
by the Korean "comfort women."

Fueled by their courage, in 1992,
she revealed her past in Tokyo
for the first time and let the world
know of the Japanese Imperial Army's
war crimes.

In 2007, she testified with Grandmothers
Kim Gun-ja and Lee Yong-soo at a hearing in
the United States House of Representatives.

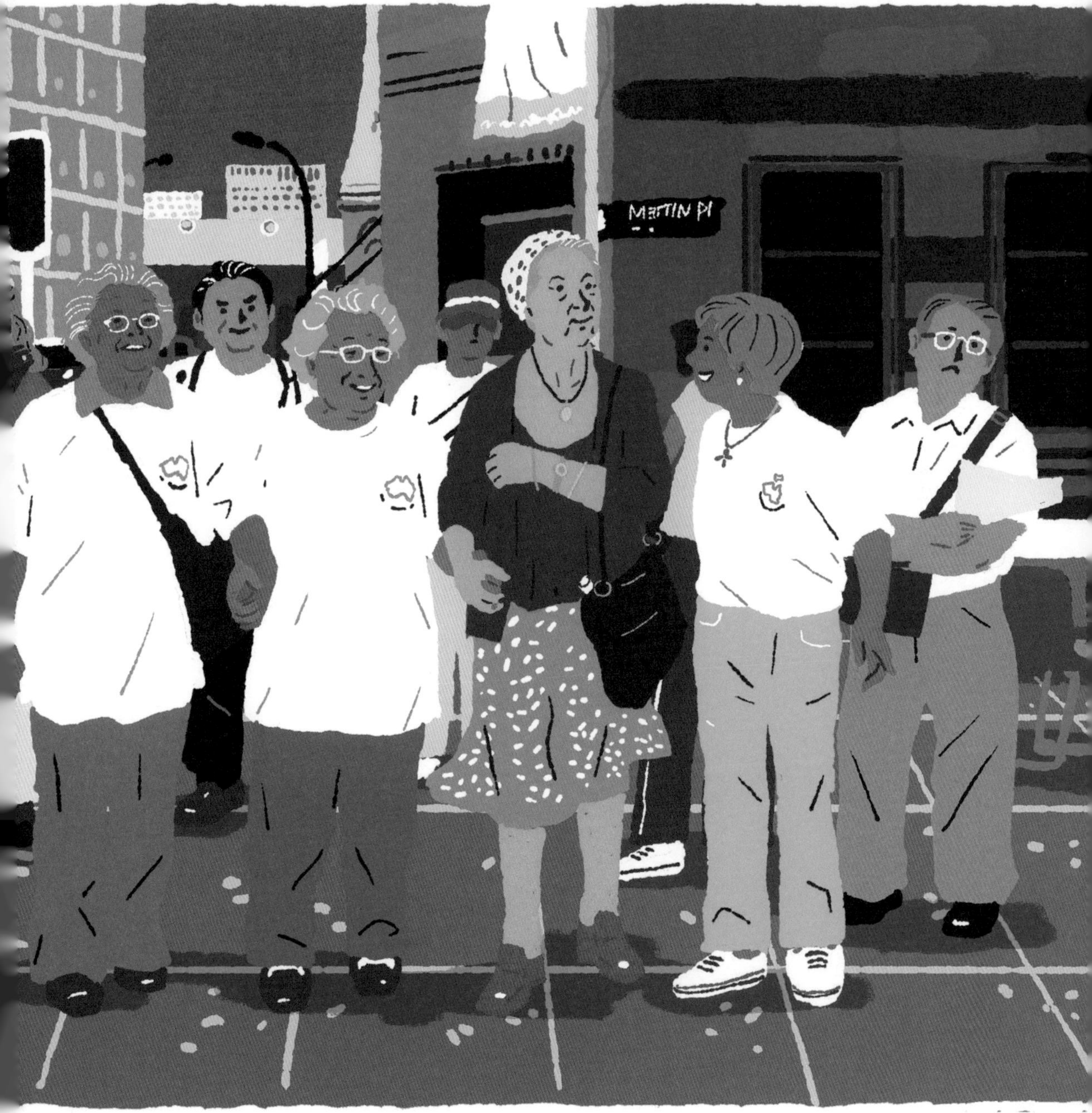
Martin Pl

The Nightmare Continues After the End of War

Thea Bisenberger-van der Wal

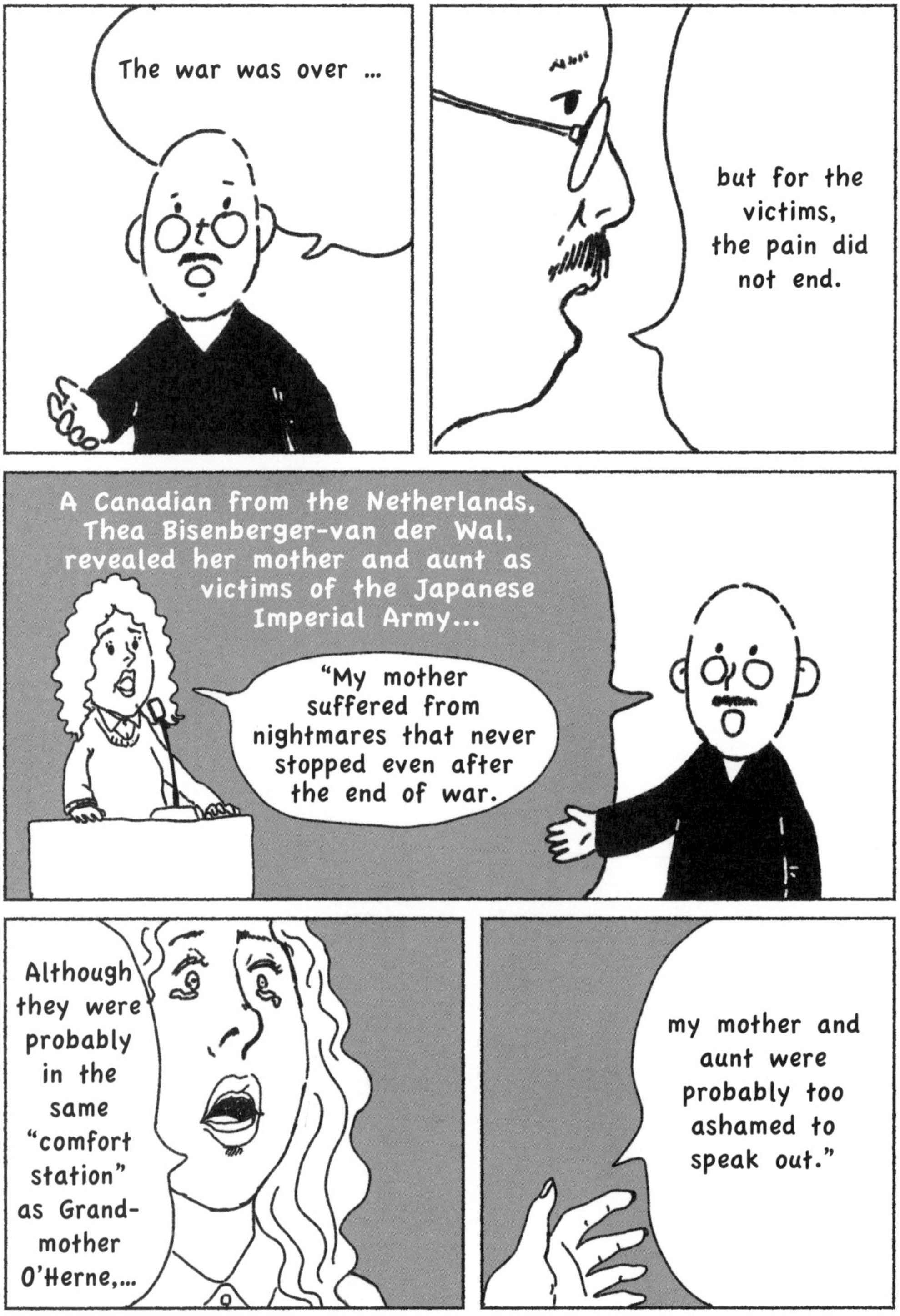
The war was over ...
but for the victims, the pain did not end.
A Canadian from the Netherlands, Thea Bisenberger-van der Wal, revealed her mother and aunt as victims of the Japanese Imperial Army...
"My mother suffered from nightmares that never stopped even after the end of war.
Although they were probably in the same "comfort station" as Grand-mother O'Herne,...
my mother and aunt were probably too ashamed to speak out."

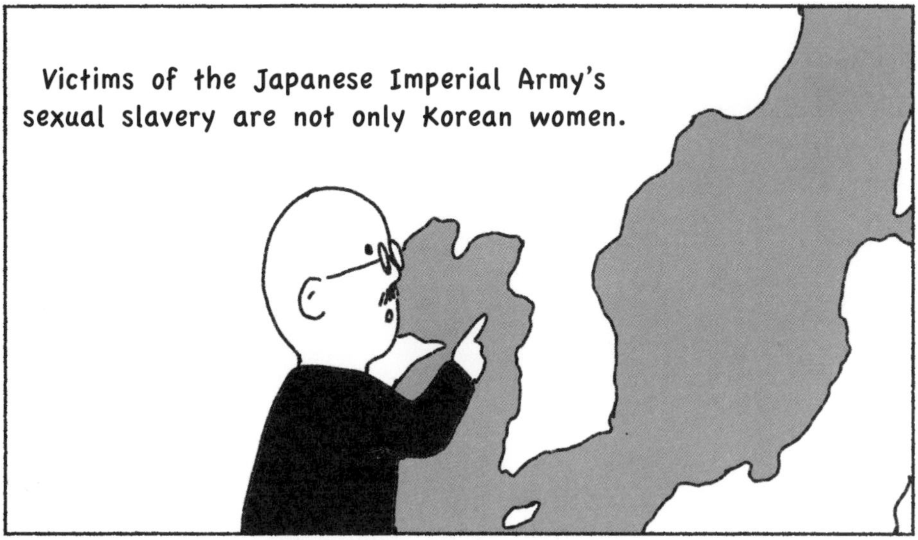
Victims of the Japanese Imperial Army's sexual slavery are not only Korean women.

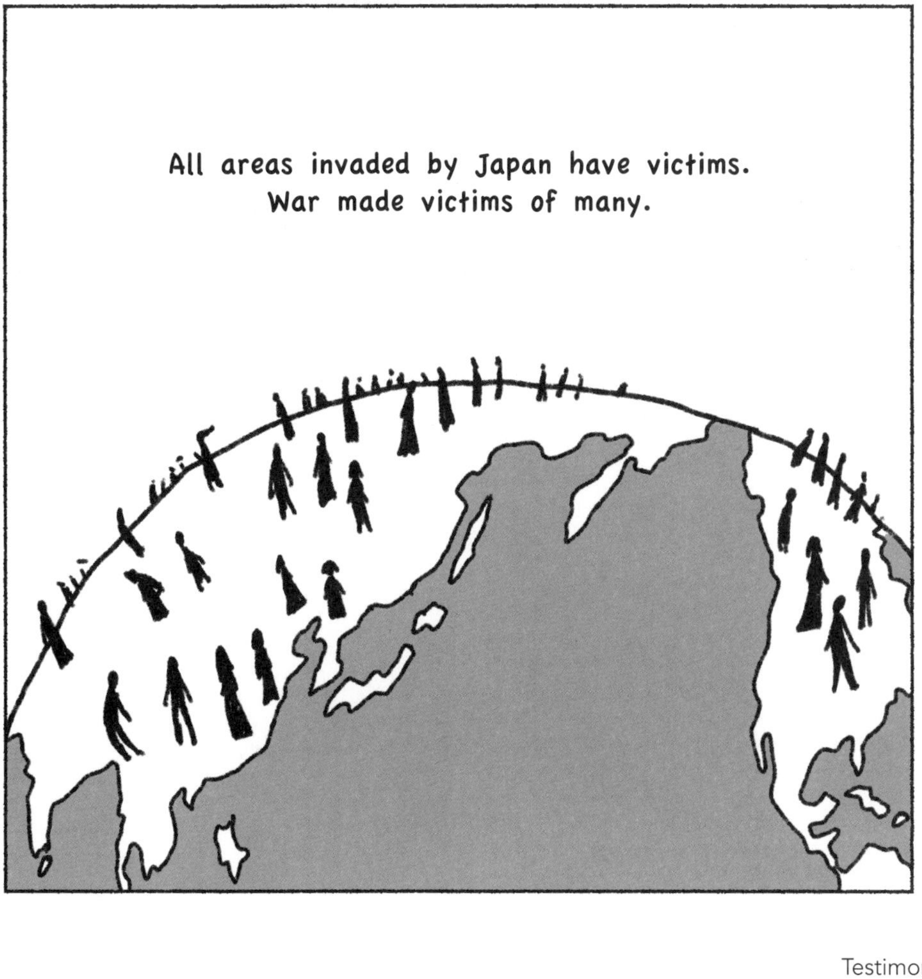
All areas invaded by Japan have victims.
War made victims of many.

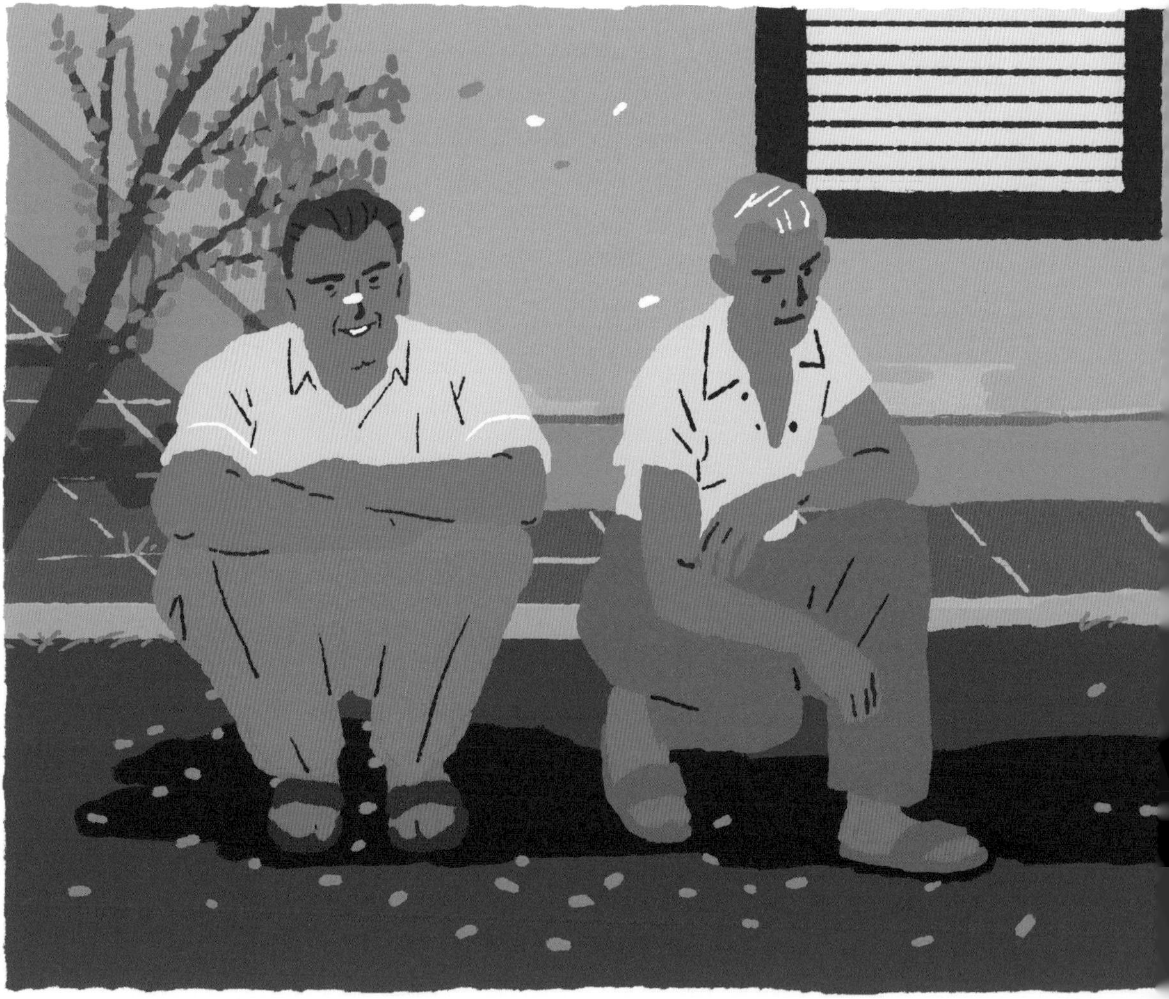

"Mother and my aunt never revealed their past as 'comfort women'.

The only person who knew was my younger aunt, who told me in 2009.

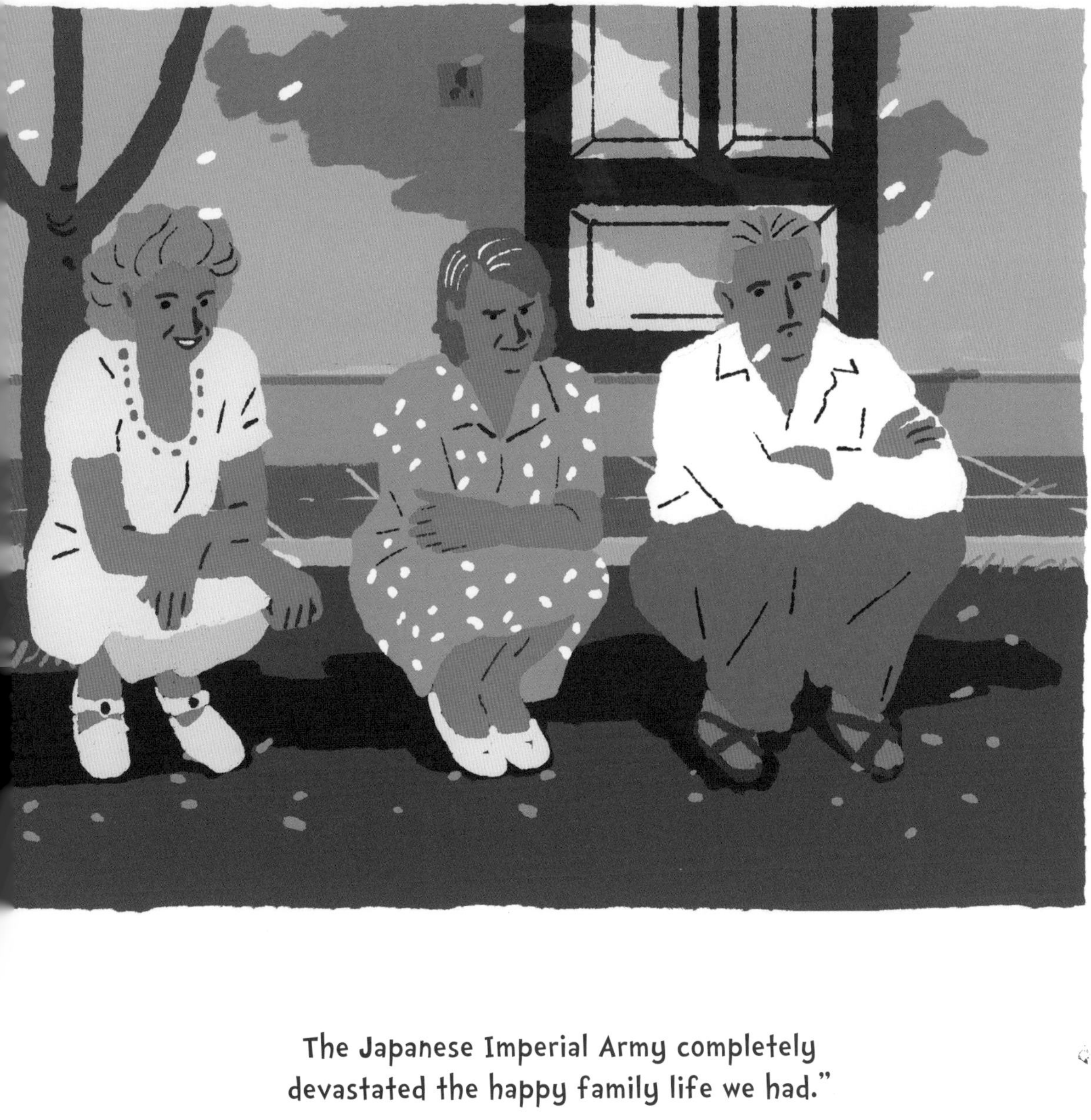

The Japanese Imperial Army completely devastated the happy family life we had."

This testimony by Thea Bisenberger-van der Wal shows how extremely painful it is for our Grandmothers to reveal their past as "comfort women."

I Am Not a "Comfort Woman"!

Grandmother Lee Ok-seon.

Why am I a "comfort woman"?
I am not.
I am Lee Ok-seon.

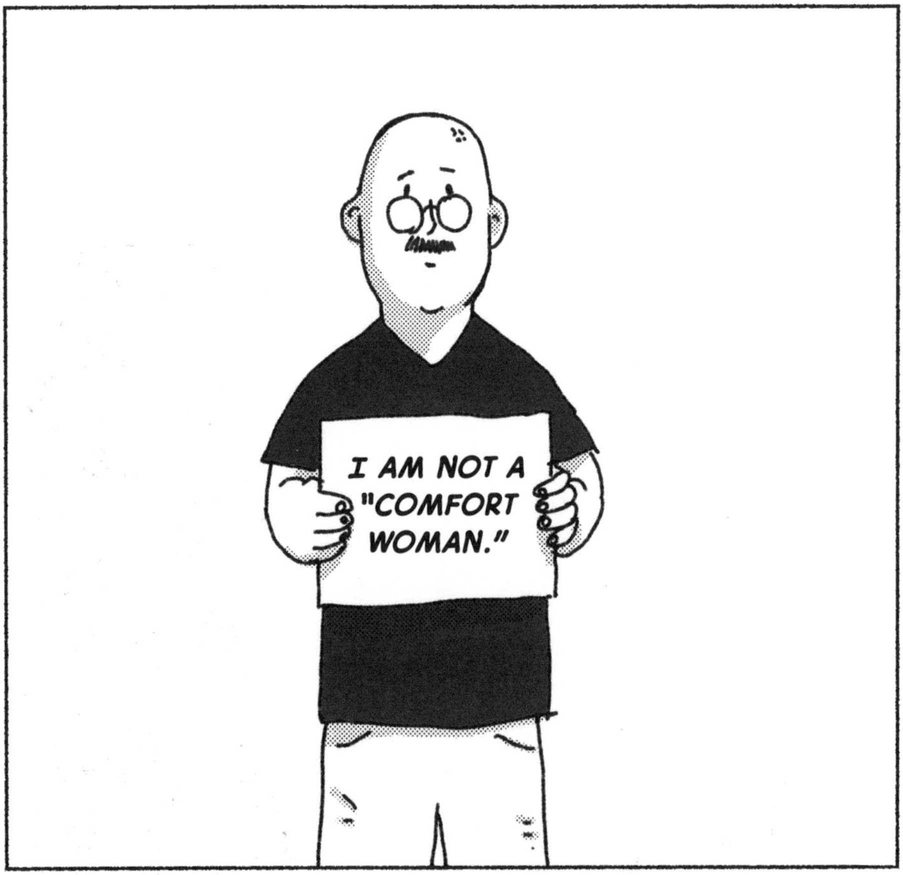
I AM NOT A "COMFORT WOMAN."

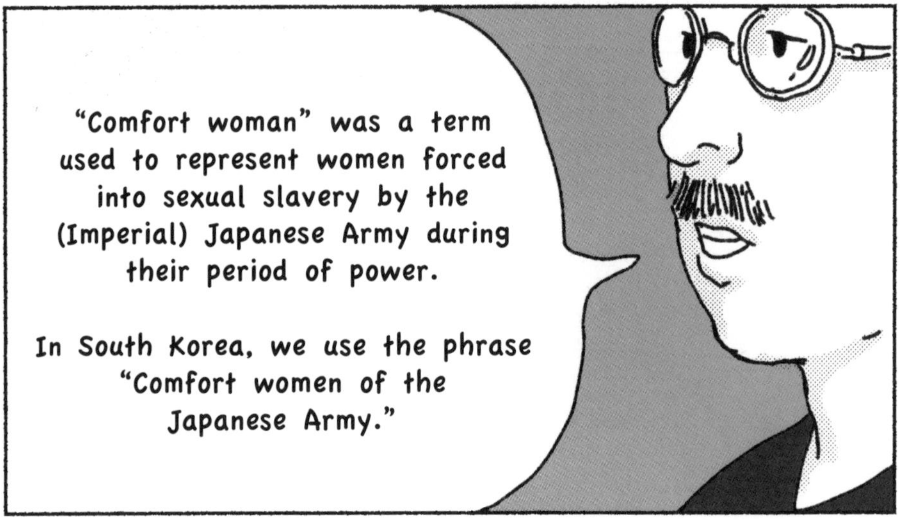
"Comfort woman" was a term used to represent women forced into sexual slavery by the (Imperial) Japanese Army during their period of power.
In South Korea, we use the phrase "Comfort women of the Japanese Army."

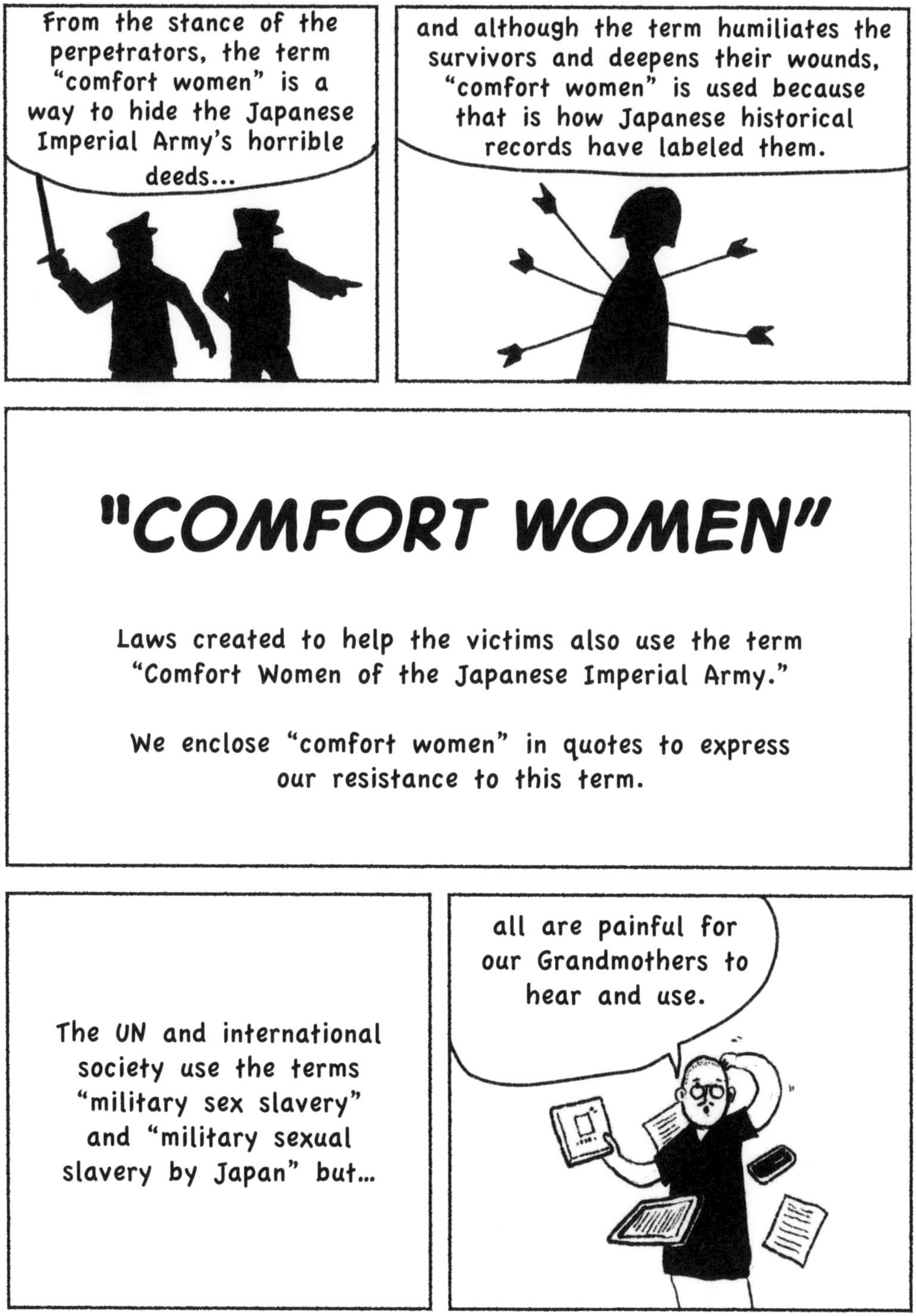
From the stance of the perpetrators, the term "comfort women" is a way to hide the Japanese Imperial Army's horrible deeds...
and although the term humiliates the survivors and deepens their wounds, "comfort women" is used because that is how Japanese historical records have labeled them.
"COMFORT WOMEN"
Laws created to help the victims also use the term "Comfort Women of the Japanese Imperial Army."
We enclose "comfort women" in quotes to express our resistance to this term.
The UN and international society use the terms "military sex slavery" and "military sexual slavery by Japan" but...
all are painful for our Grandmothers to hear and use.

The Grandmothers—whose feelings should matter the most—
do not want to be called
"comfort women," "sexual slaves," and "victims."

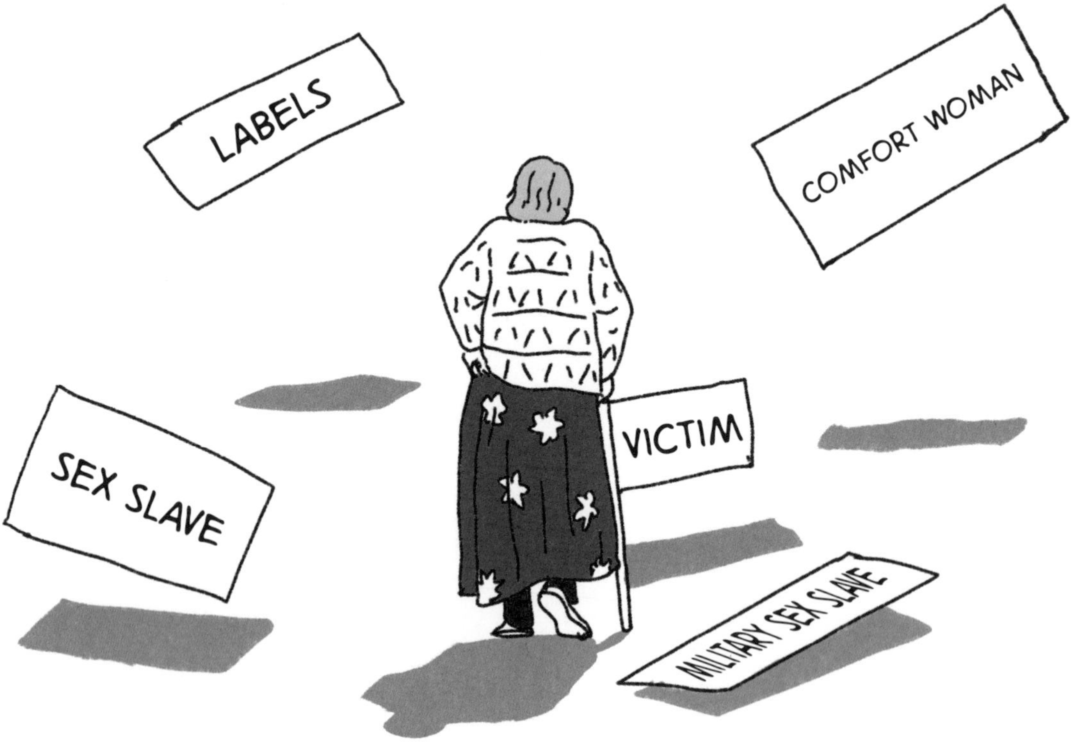
LABELS
COMFORT WOMAN
SEX SLAVE
VICTIM
MILITARY SEX SLAVE

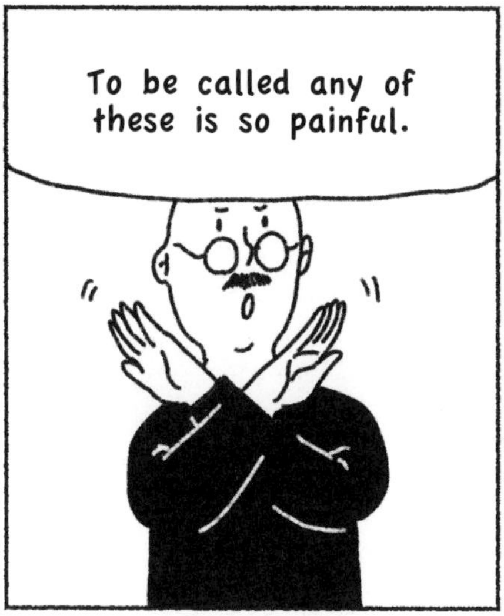
To be called any of these is so painful.

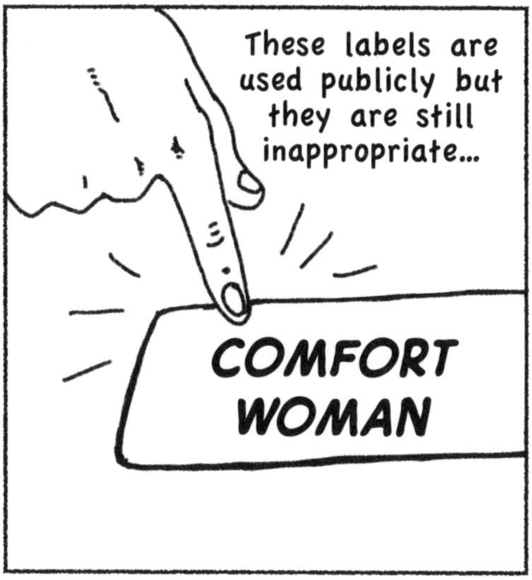
These labels are used publicly but they are still inappropriate...
COMFORT WOMAN

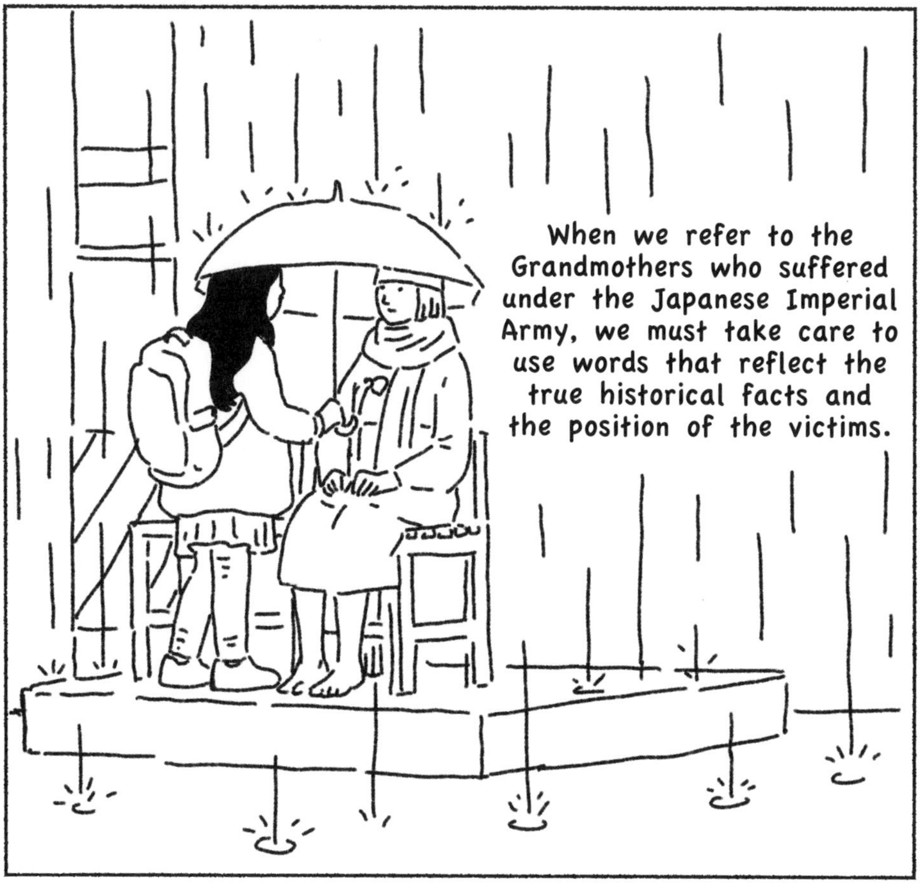
When we refer to the Grandmothers who suffered under the Japanese Imperial Army, we must take care to use words that reflect the true historical facts and the position of the victims.

CHAPTER 2

Memories

Where There Are Songs There Is Laughter

Grandmother Gil Won-ok

Grandmother, I like your singing. I feel
happy just listening to you and many
thoughts pass through my head.

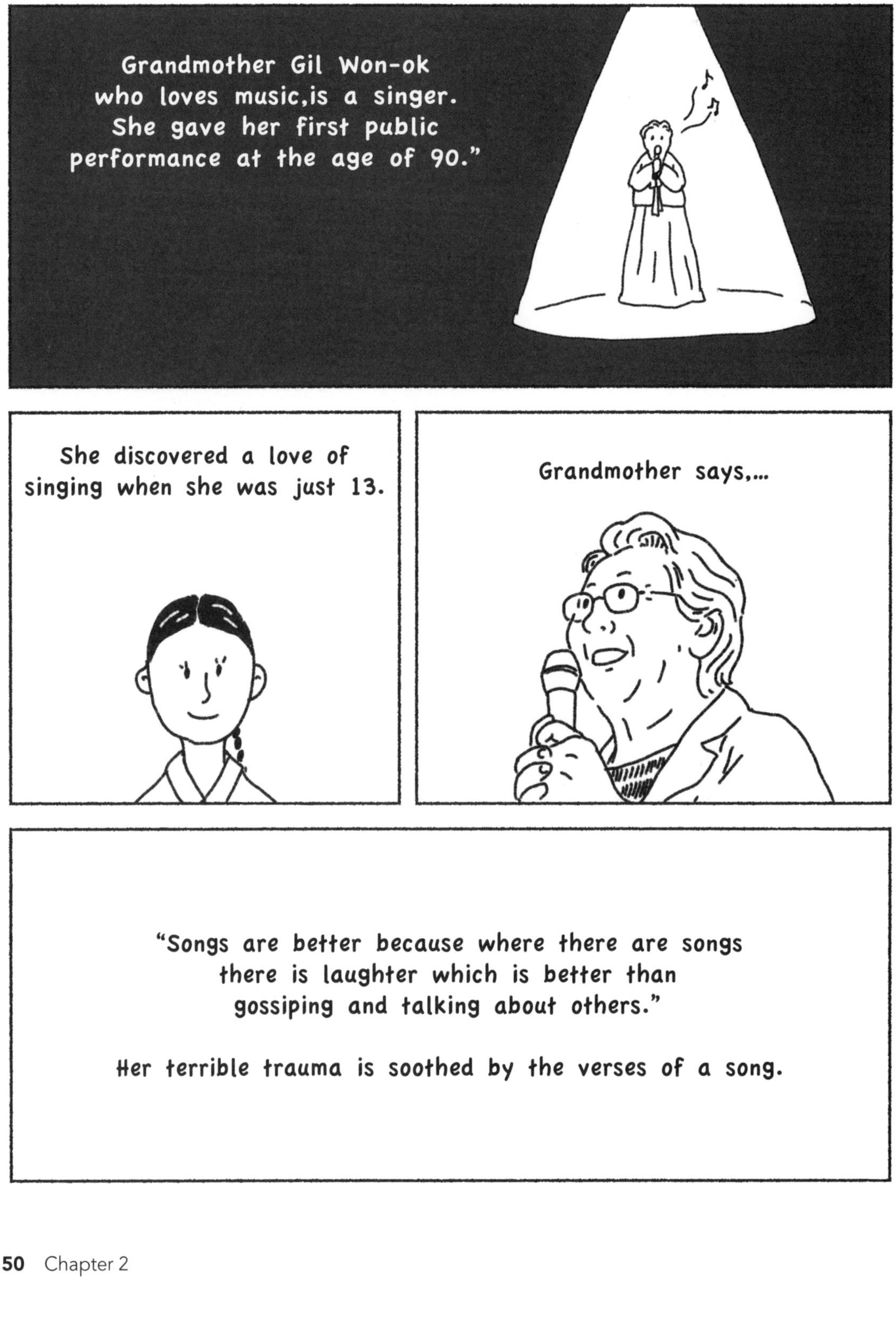
Grandmother Gil Won-ok who loves music,is a singer. She gave her first public performance at the age of 90."
She discovered a love of singing when she was just 13.
Grandmother says,...
"Songs are better because where there are songs there is laughter which is better than gossiping and talking about others."
Her terrible trauma is soothed by the verses of a song.

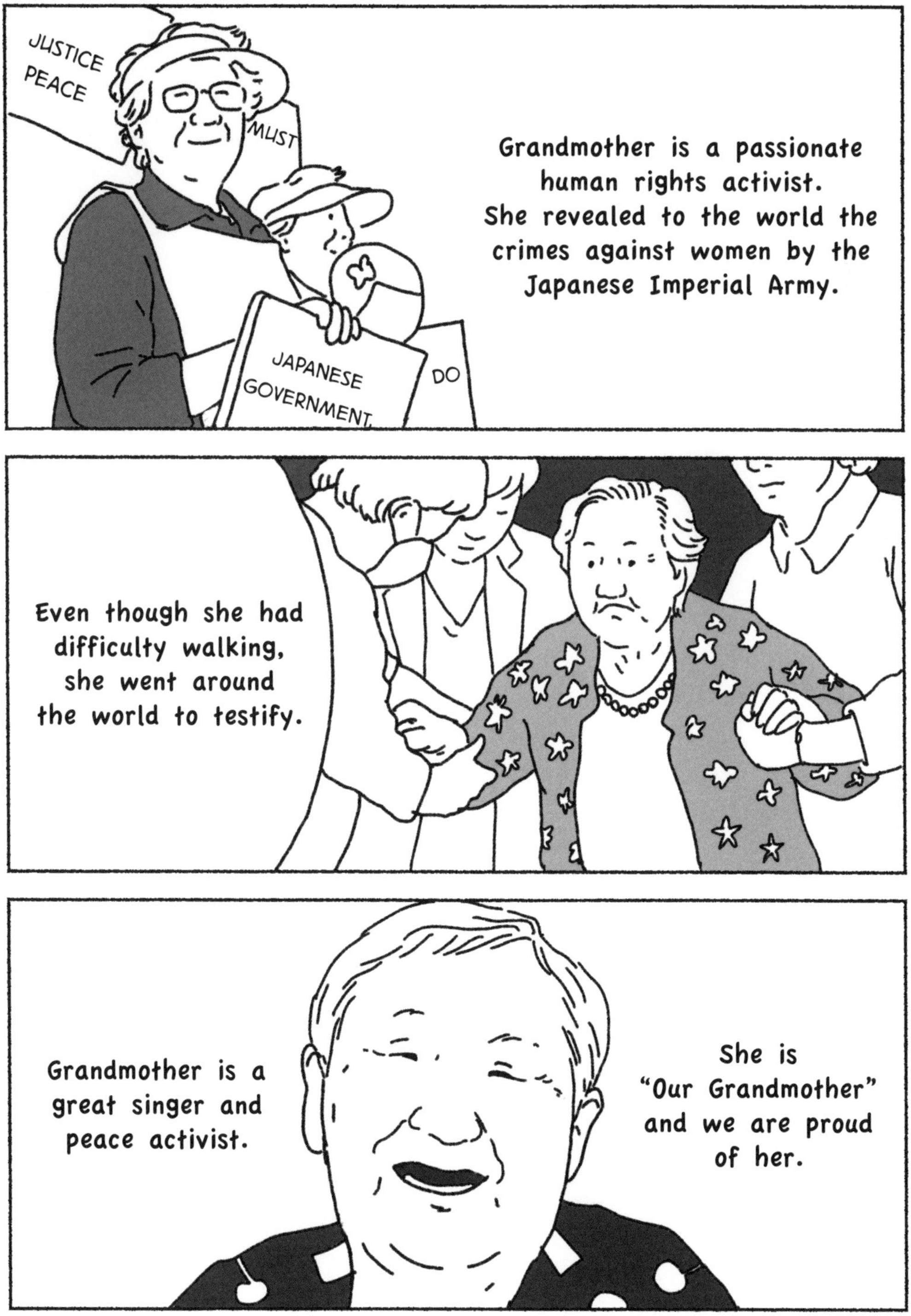
JUSTICE
PEACE
MUST
JAPANESE GOVERNMENT
DO
Grandmother is a passionate human rights activist. She revealed to the world the crimes against women by the Japanese Imperial Army.
Even though she had difficulty walking, she went around the world to testify.
Grandmother is a great singer and peace activist.
She is "Our Grandmother" and we are proud of her.

Toward Home, Toward the South

Grandmother Choi Gab-soon

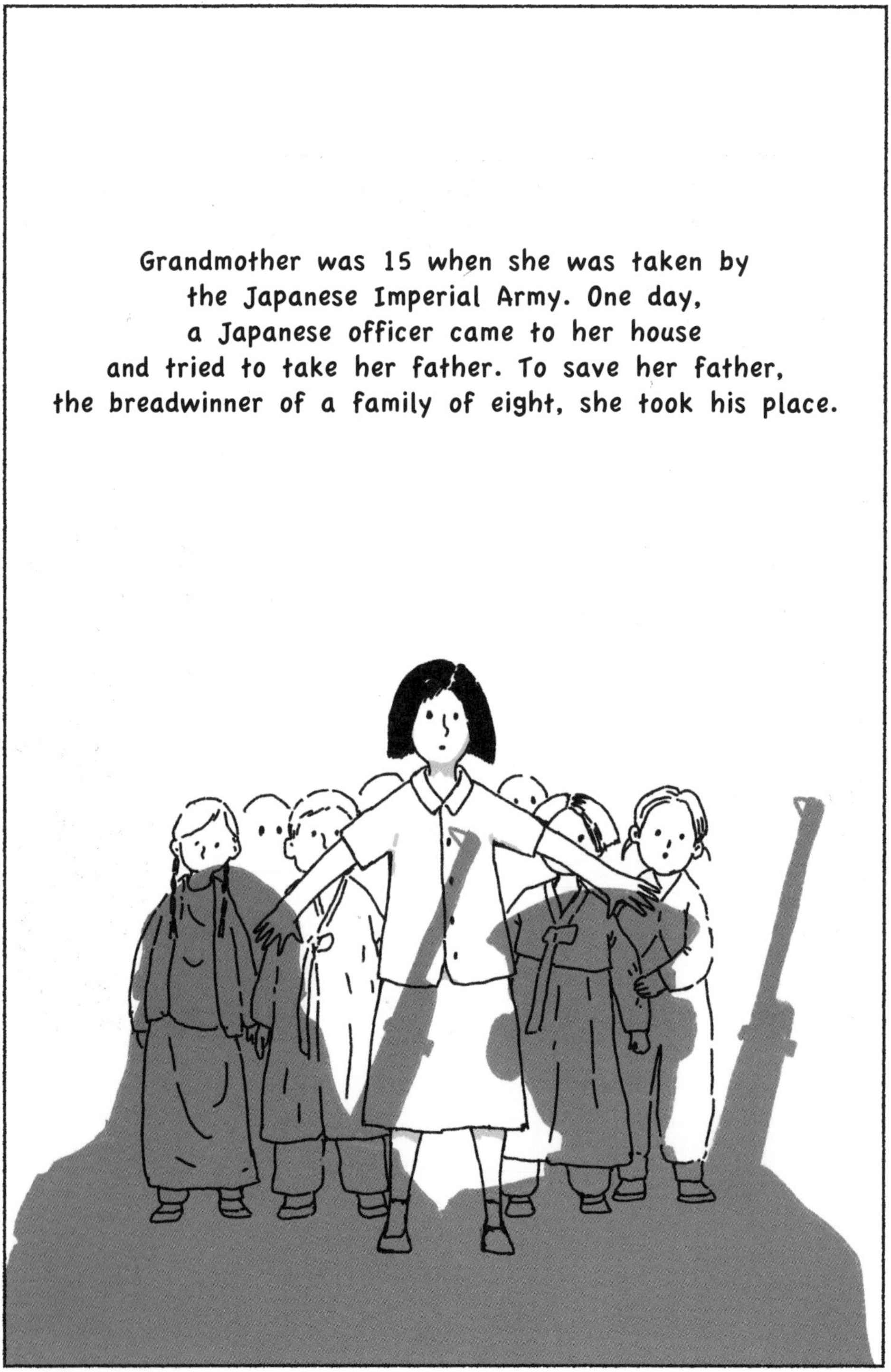
Grandmother was 15 when she was taken by the Japanese Imperial Army. One day, a Japanese officer came to her house and tried to take her father. To save her father, the breadwinner of a family of eight, she took his place.

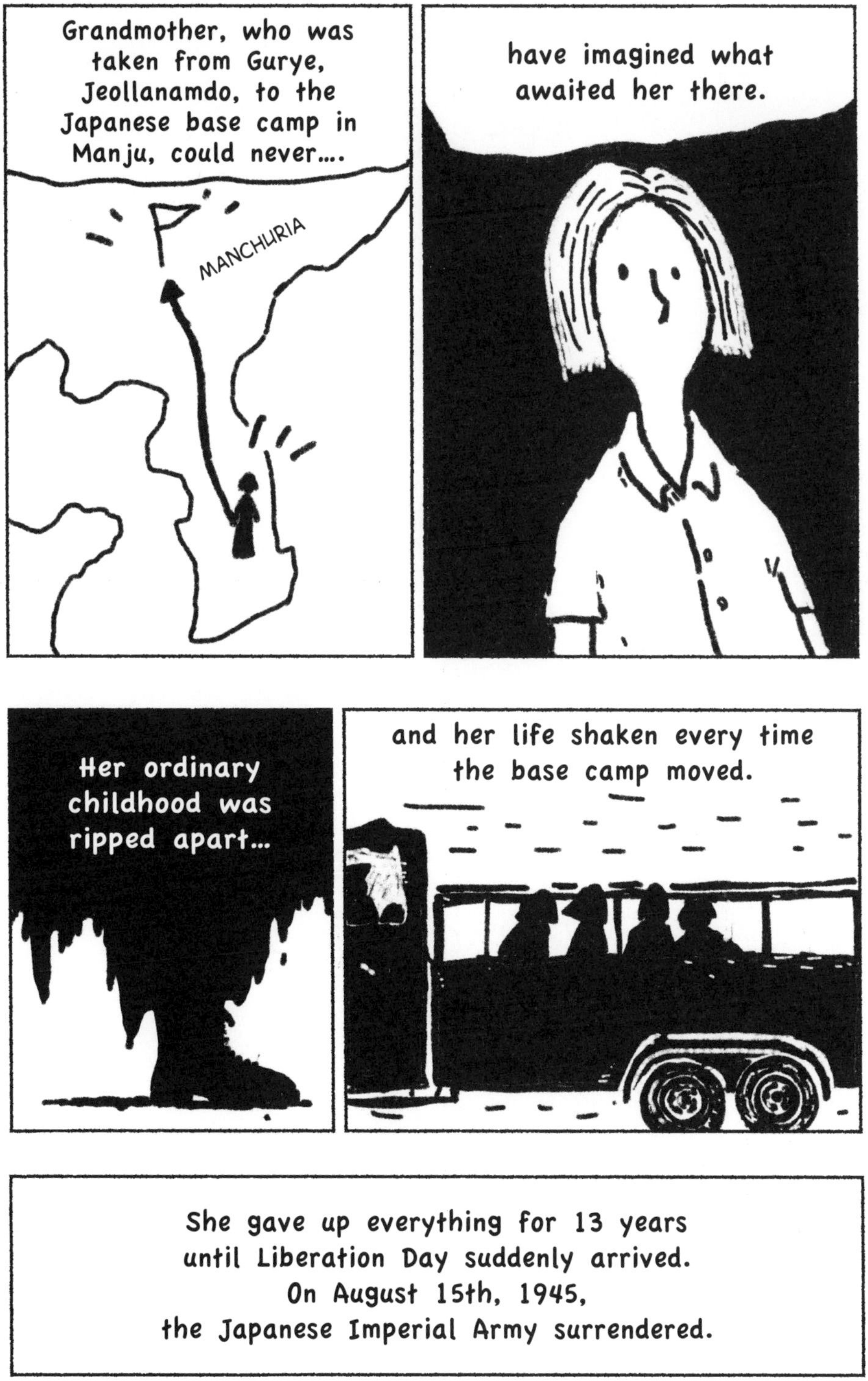
Grandmother, who was taken from Gurye, Jeollanamdo, to the Japanese base camp in Manju, could never....
MANCHURIA
have imagined what awaited her there.
Her ordinary childhood was ripped apart...
and her life shaken every time the base camp moved.
She gave up everything for 13 years until Liberation Day suddenly arrived. On August 15th, 1945, the Japanese Imperial Army surrendered.

She missed home so much...

but Grandmother
could not return.

She had no money...

and no energy.

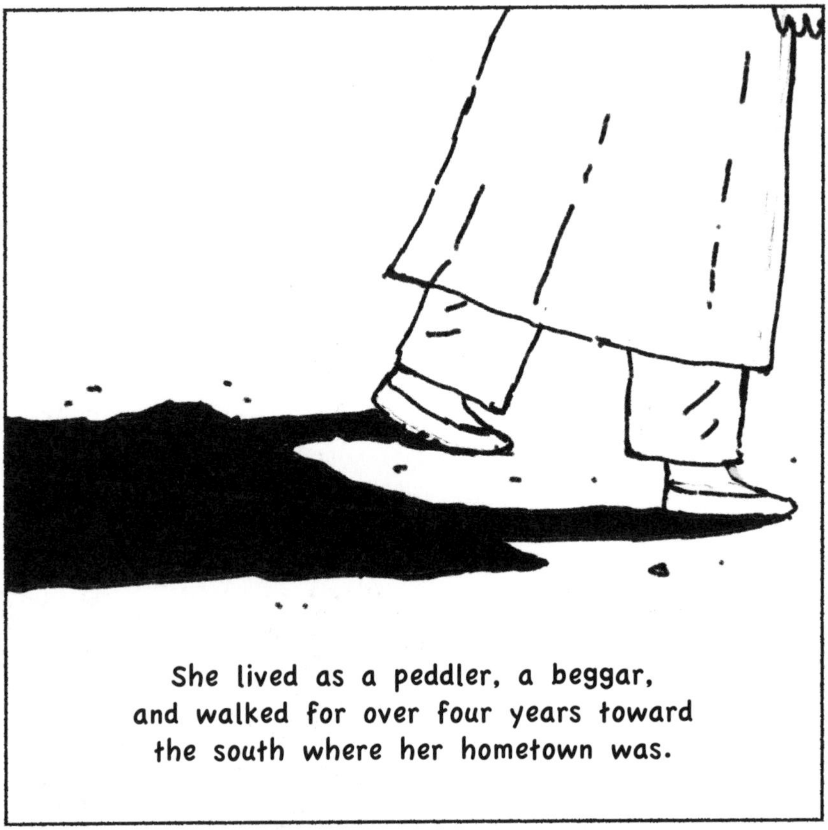
She lived as a peddler, a beggar,
and walked for over four years toward
the south where her hometown was.

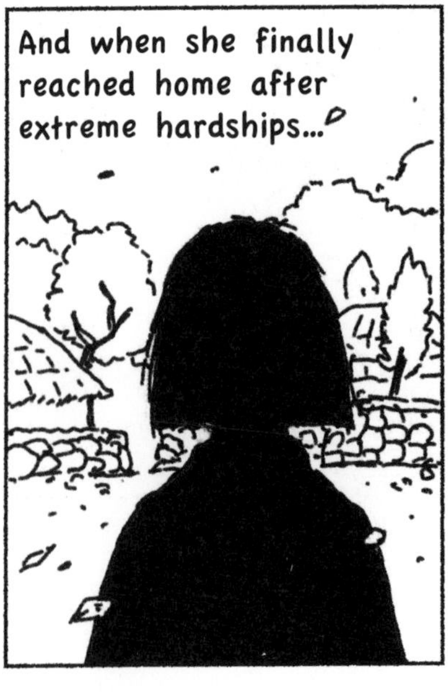
And when she finally
reached home after
extreme hardships...

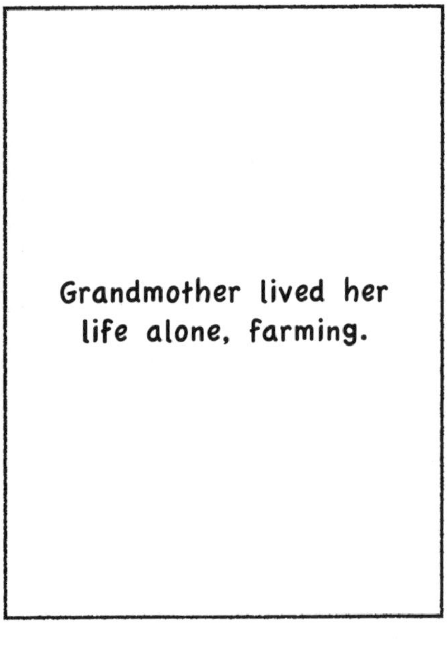
Grandmother lived her
life alone, farming.

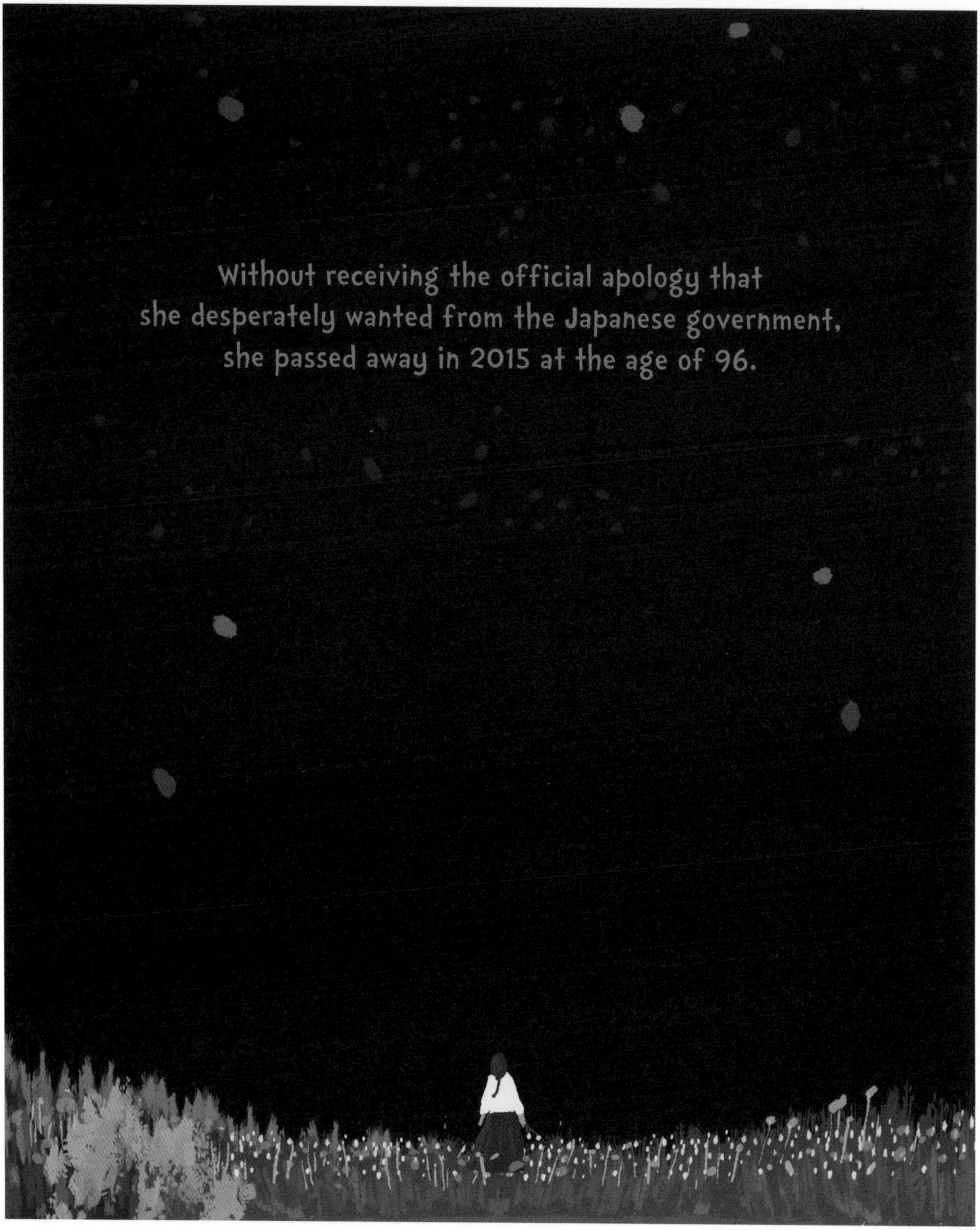
Without receiving the official apology that she desperately wanted from the Japanese government, she passed away in 2015 at the age of 96.

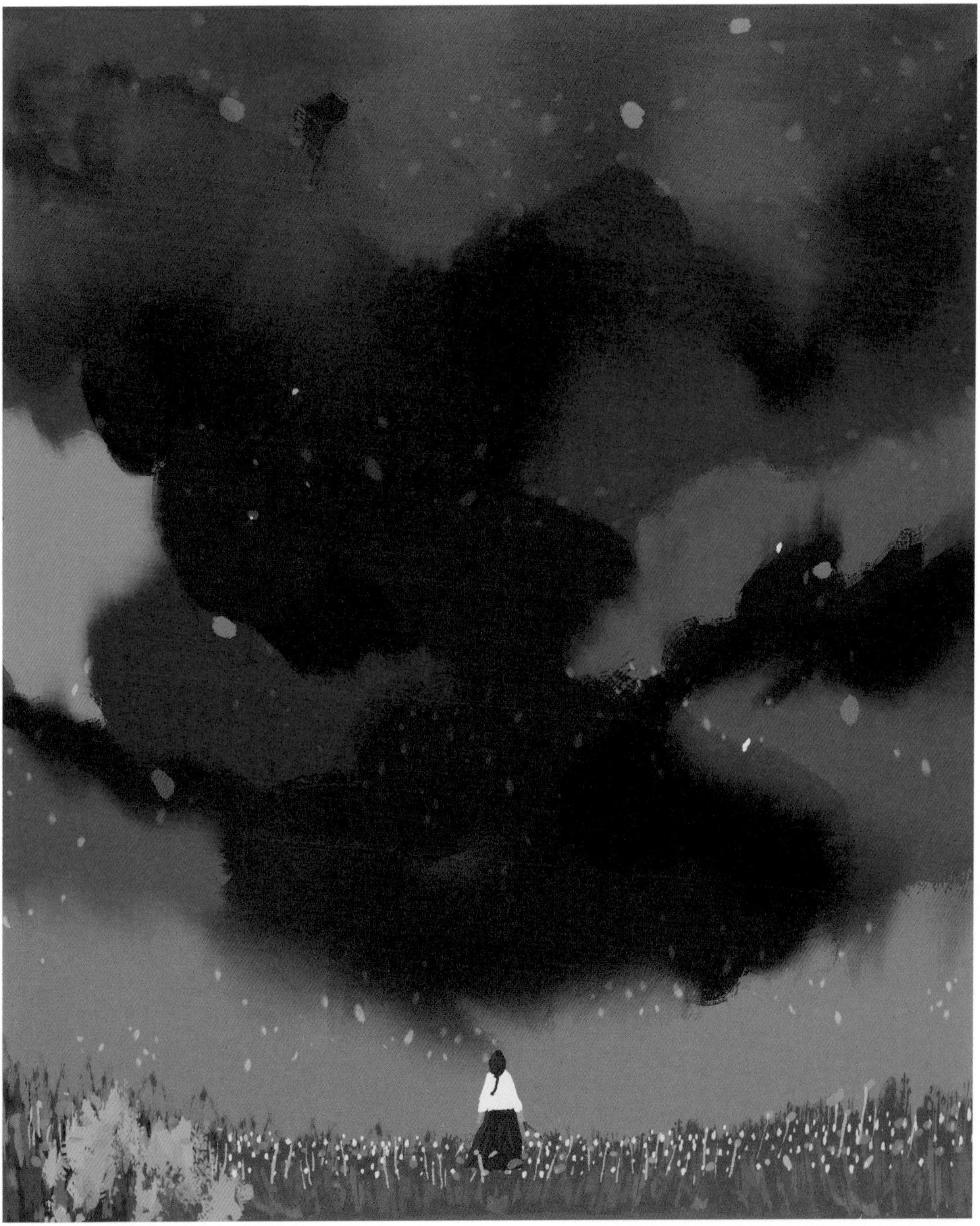

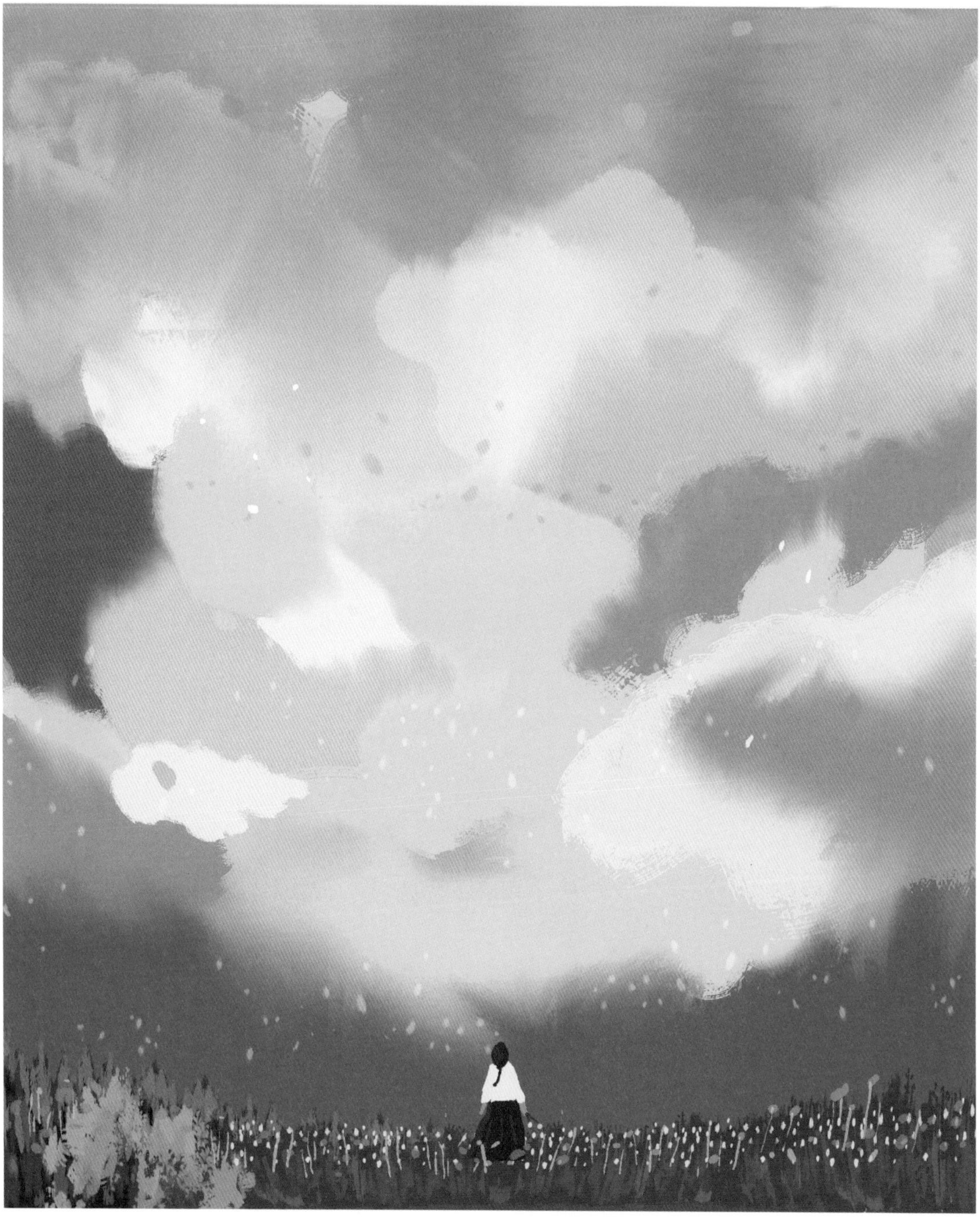

Arirang, Doraji, Mother

Grandmother Pak Cha-soon

"I remember the song. Doraji, doraji, doraji..."

*Doraji is a Korean root vegetable.

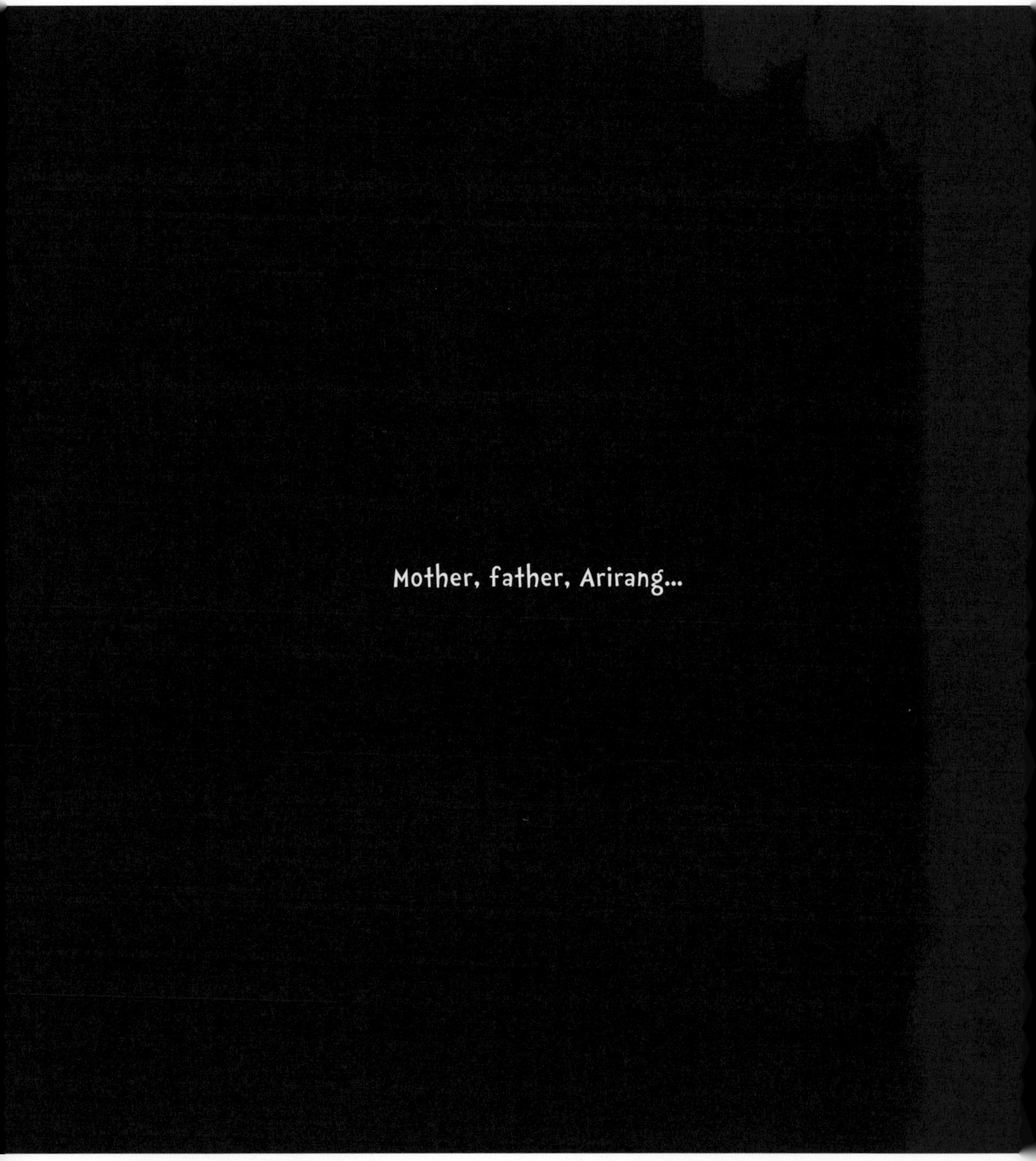
Mother, father, Arirang...

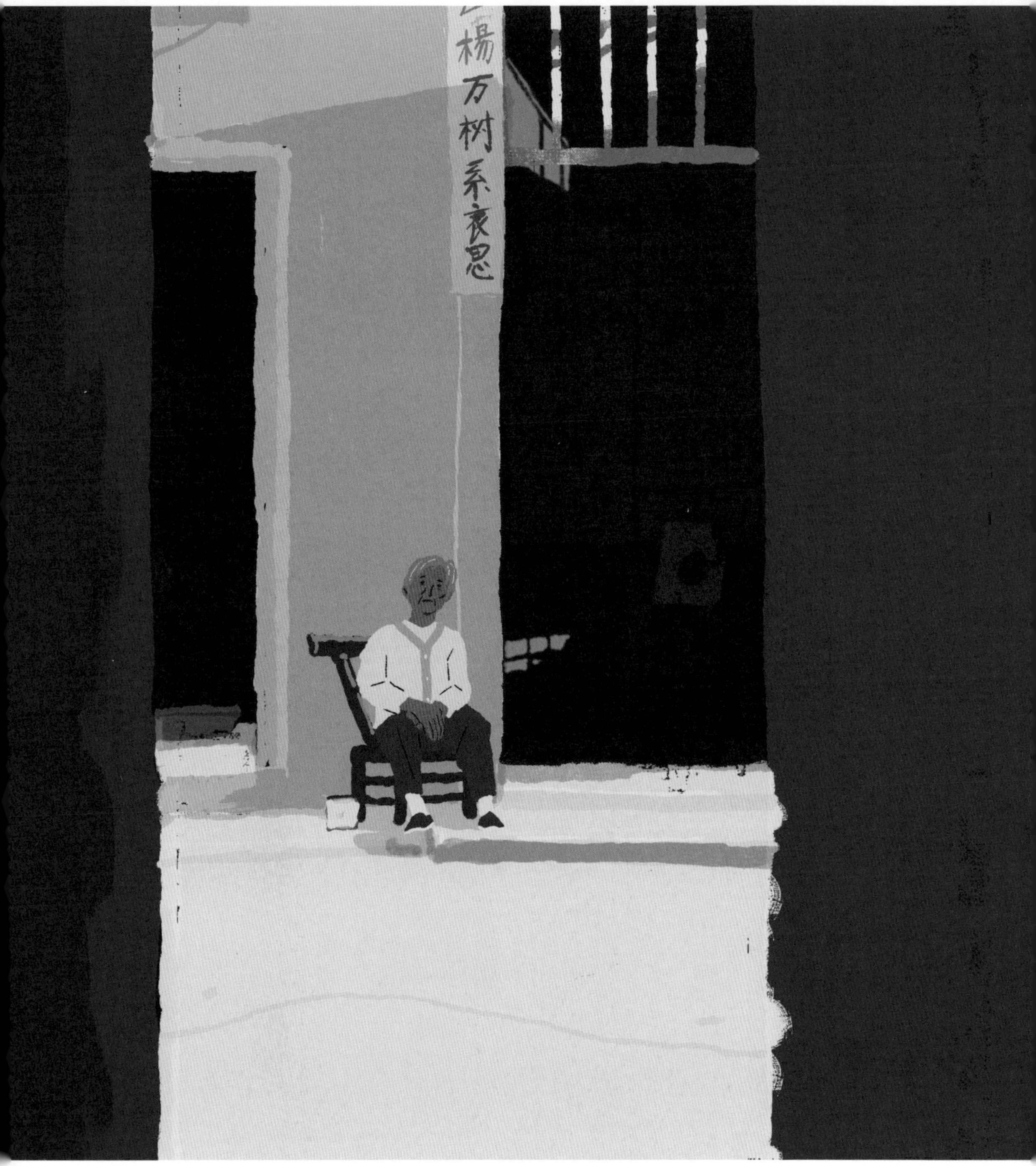
楊万树系哀思

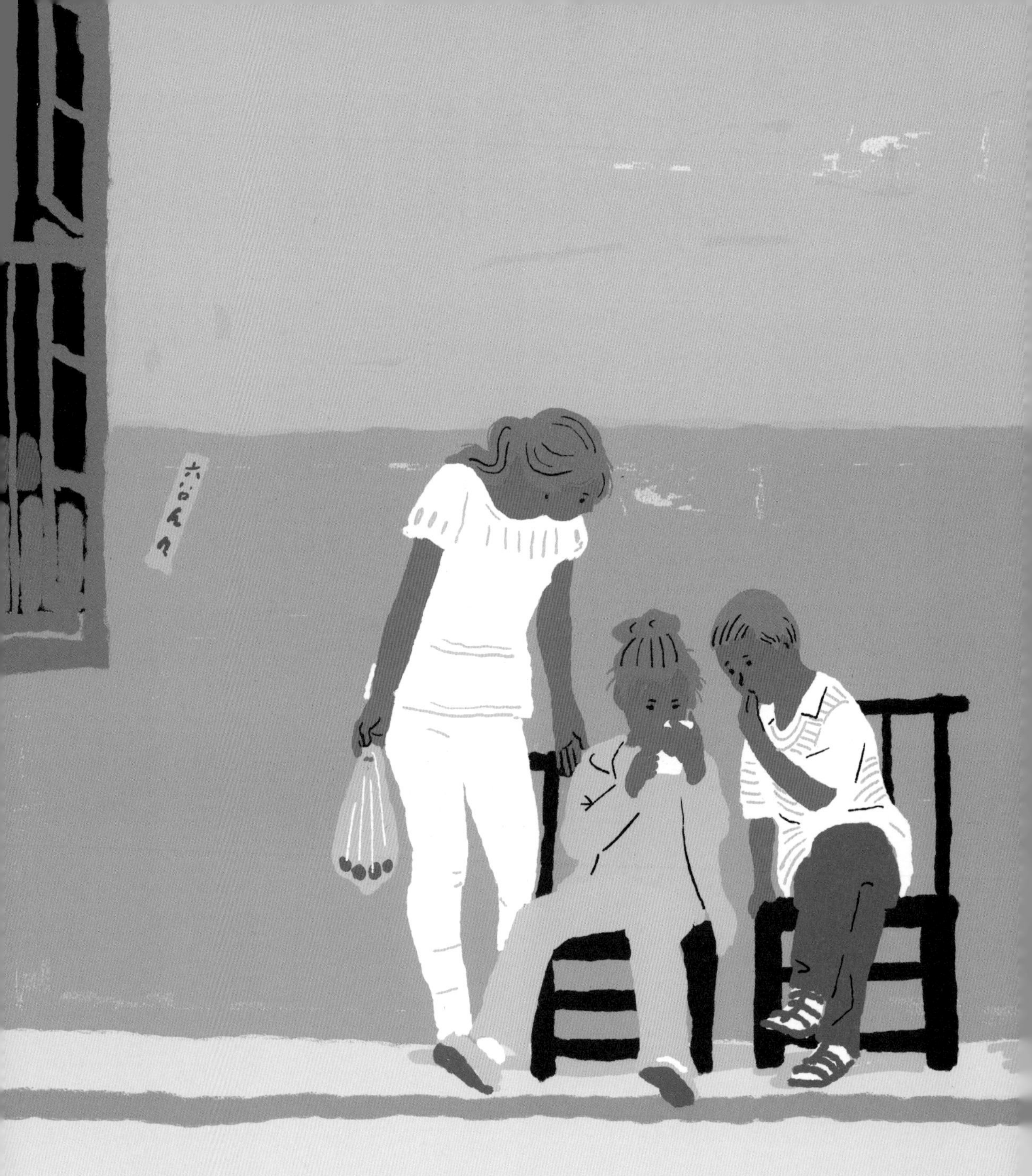

In the documentary film, 22, Grandmother Pak makes an appearance.

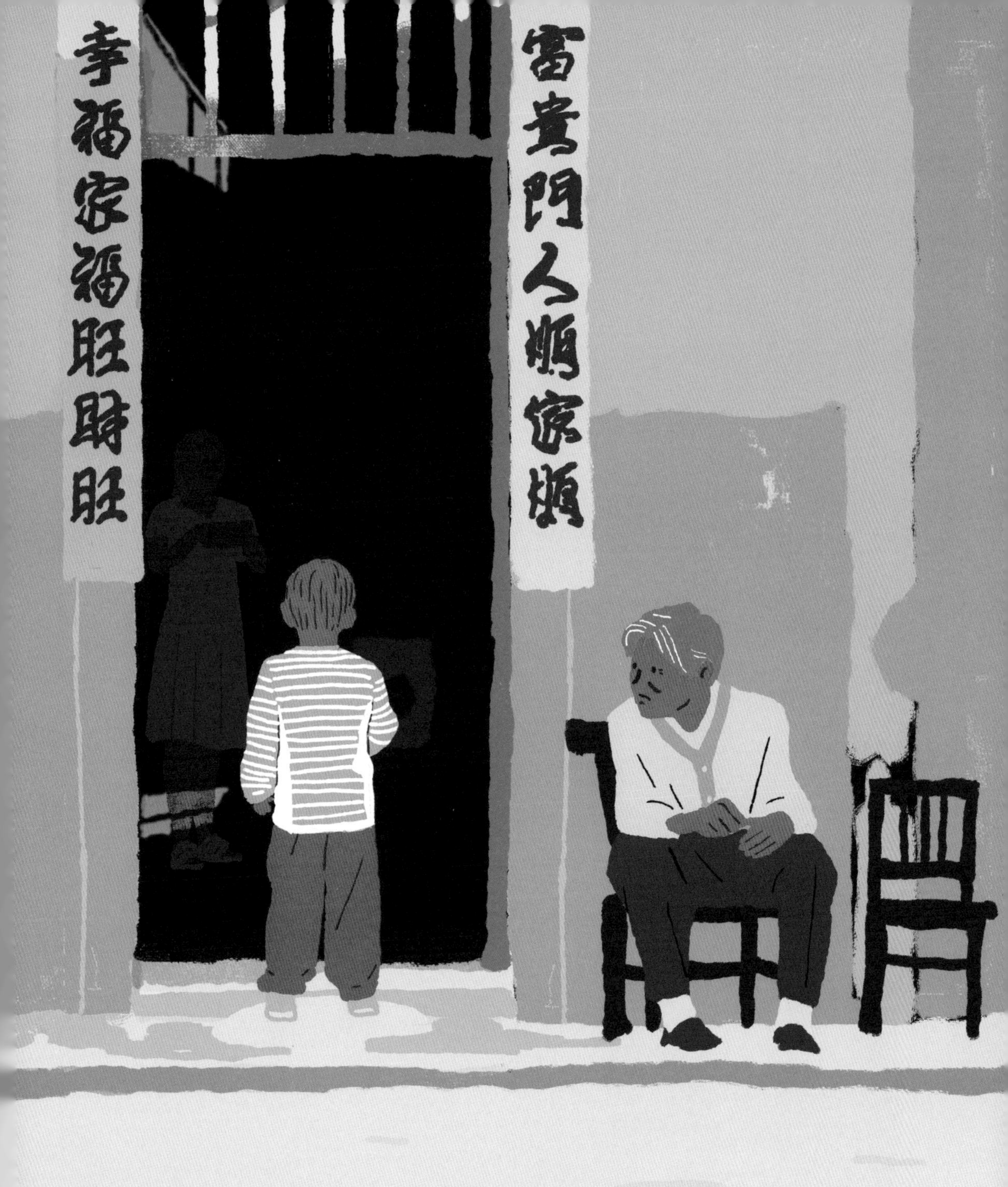

富貴門人順家順
幸福家福旺財旺

• A documentary collaboration based on Chinese "comfort women" survivors. The title 22 depicts the number of survivors as of 2014 when the documentary was filmed. (Director GUO Ke, 2015).

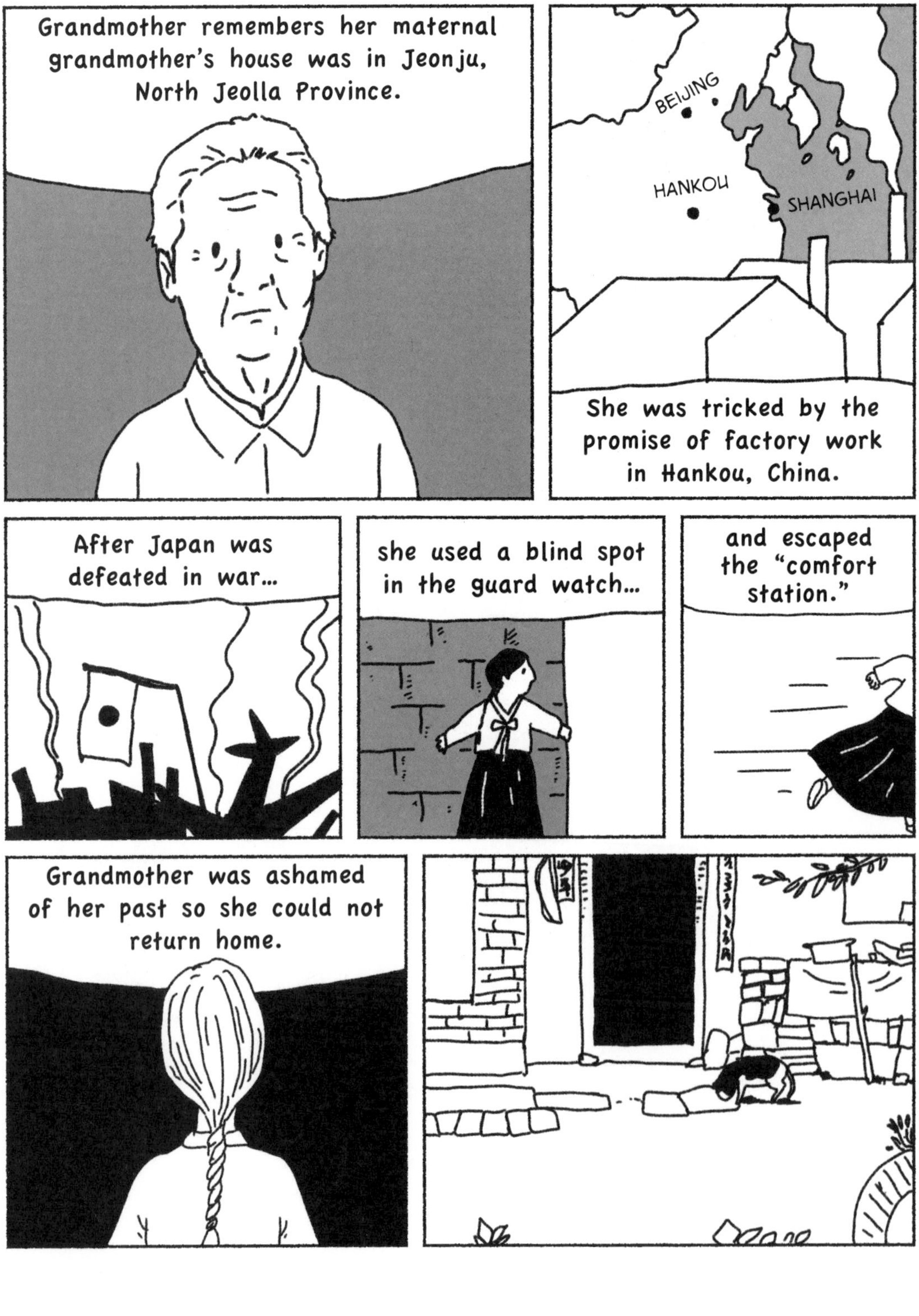
Grandmother remembers her maternal grandmother's house was in Jeonju, North Jeolla Province.
BEIJING
HANKOU
SHANGHAI
She was tricked by the promise of factory work in Hankou, China.
After Japan was defeated in war...
she used a blind spot in the guard watch...
and escaped the "comfort station."
Grandmother was ashamed of her past so she could not return home.

She married a Chinese man and adopted a two-year-old child.

Seventy-six years of living in China made her forget her Korean.

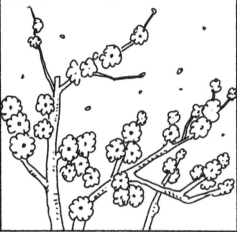

DORAJI   DORAJI

But she remembers the folk song Arirang and Doraji and the lyrics "doraji, doraji...doraji..."

ARIRANG

Grandmother may have forgotten her mother tongue but she did not forget its folksongs Arirang and Doraji.

We will remember Grandmother Pak Cha-soon who kept the old songs in her heart despite her harsh life.

When I said to her, "Grandmother, you are so pretty,"
she broke into a beautiful smile.

I Am Always by Your Side.

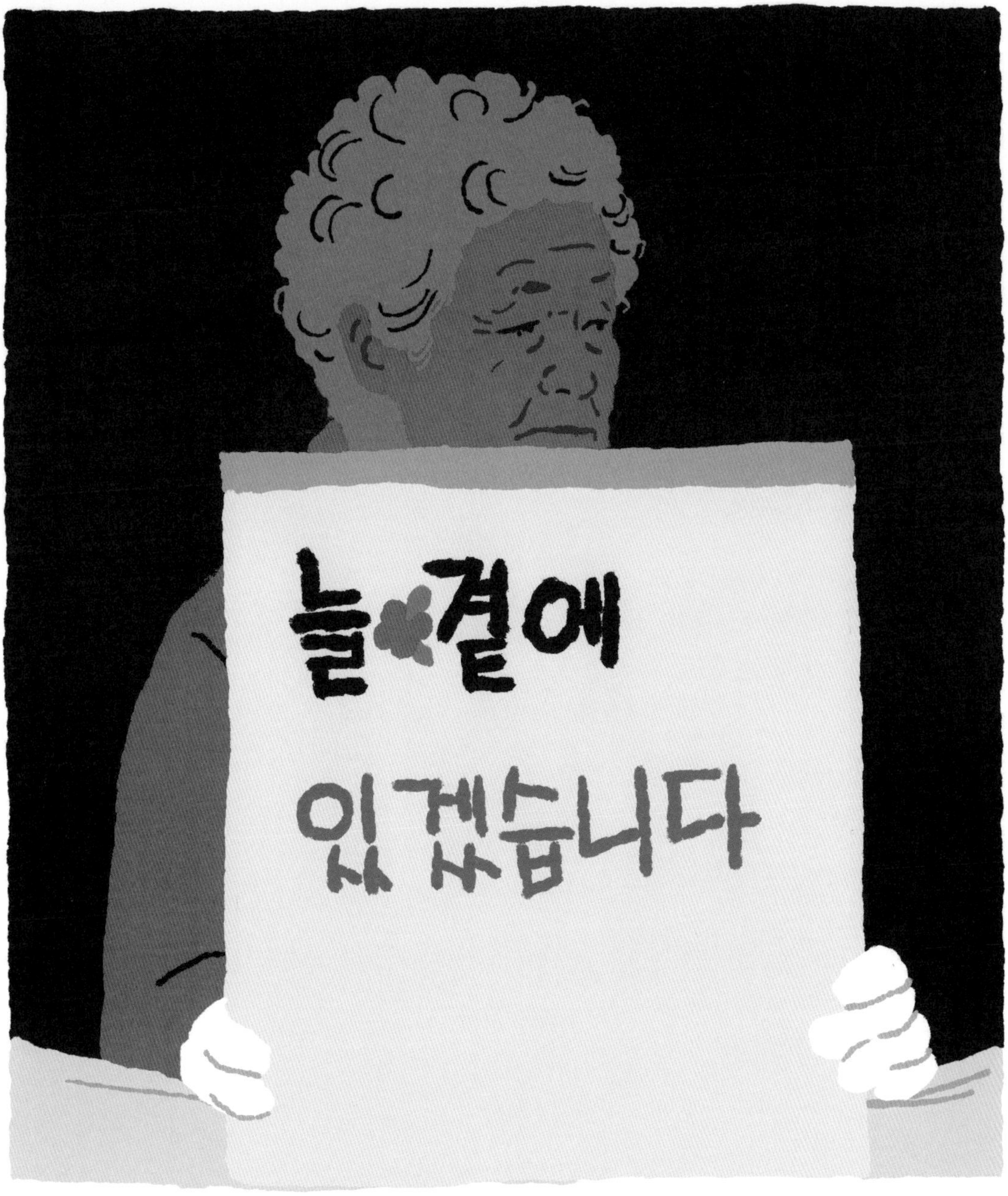
늘 곁에
있겠습니다

Grandmother Kim Eun-rye

"Be there" "Grandmother Kim Eun-rye. I am always by your side."

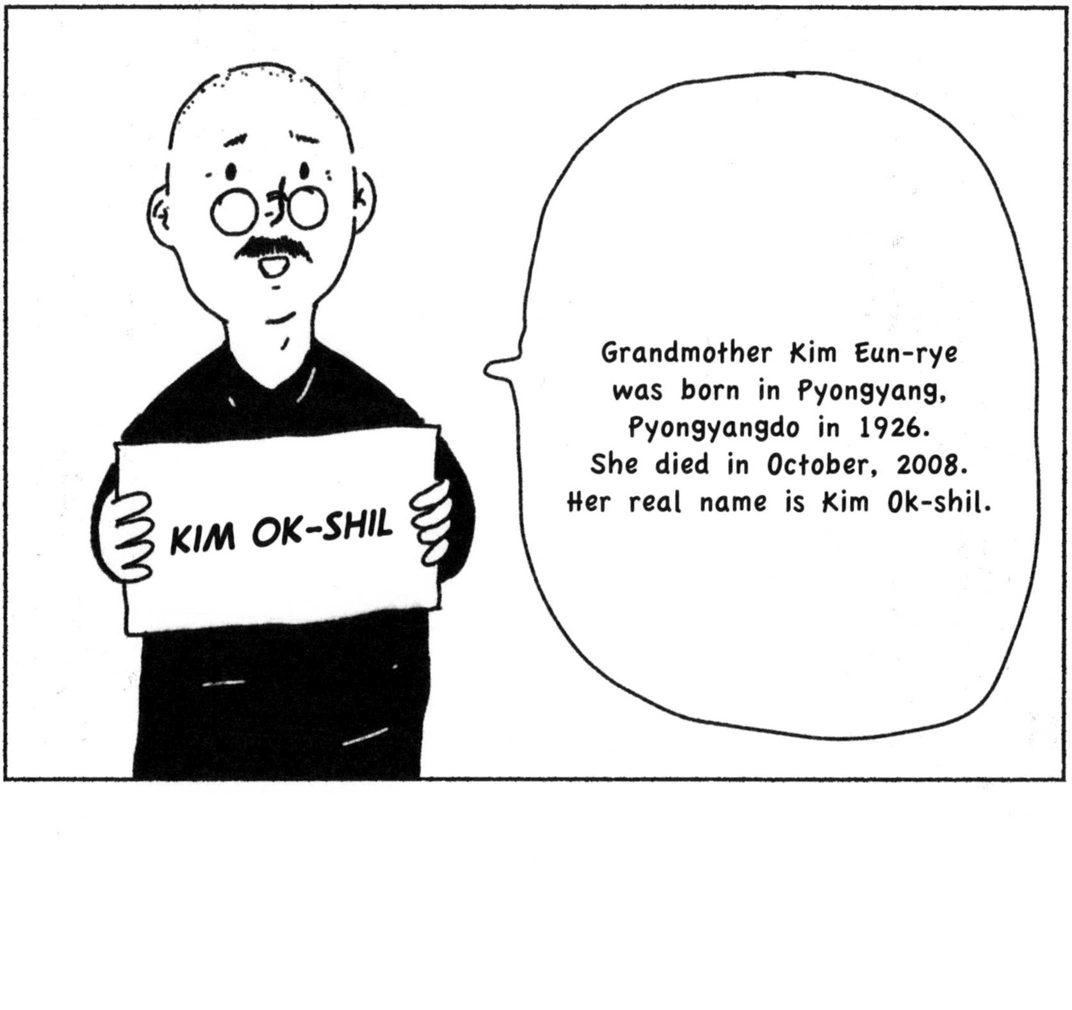
KIM OK-SHIL
Grandmother Kim Eun-rye was born in Pyongyang, Pyongyangdo in 1926. She died in October, 2008. Her real name is Kim Ok-shil.

After liberation, she returned to Korea but she could not return home. The name "Eun-rye" became her official name on the hojok.

Some grandmothers forget...

memories...

names...

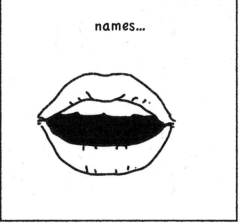

and their mother tongue.

• The hojok is the family name document that contains the person's birth town, name, and date of birth. With the abolition of the hojok law, the family relation records took its place.

The movie Mary Poppins made me think of Grandmother.
Like the scene where Mary Poppins comes down with her umbrella,
I wished there was some kind of magic in our world.

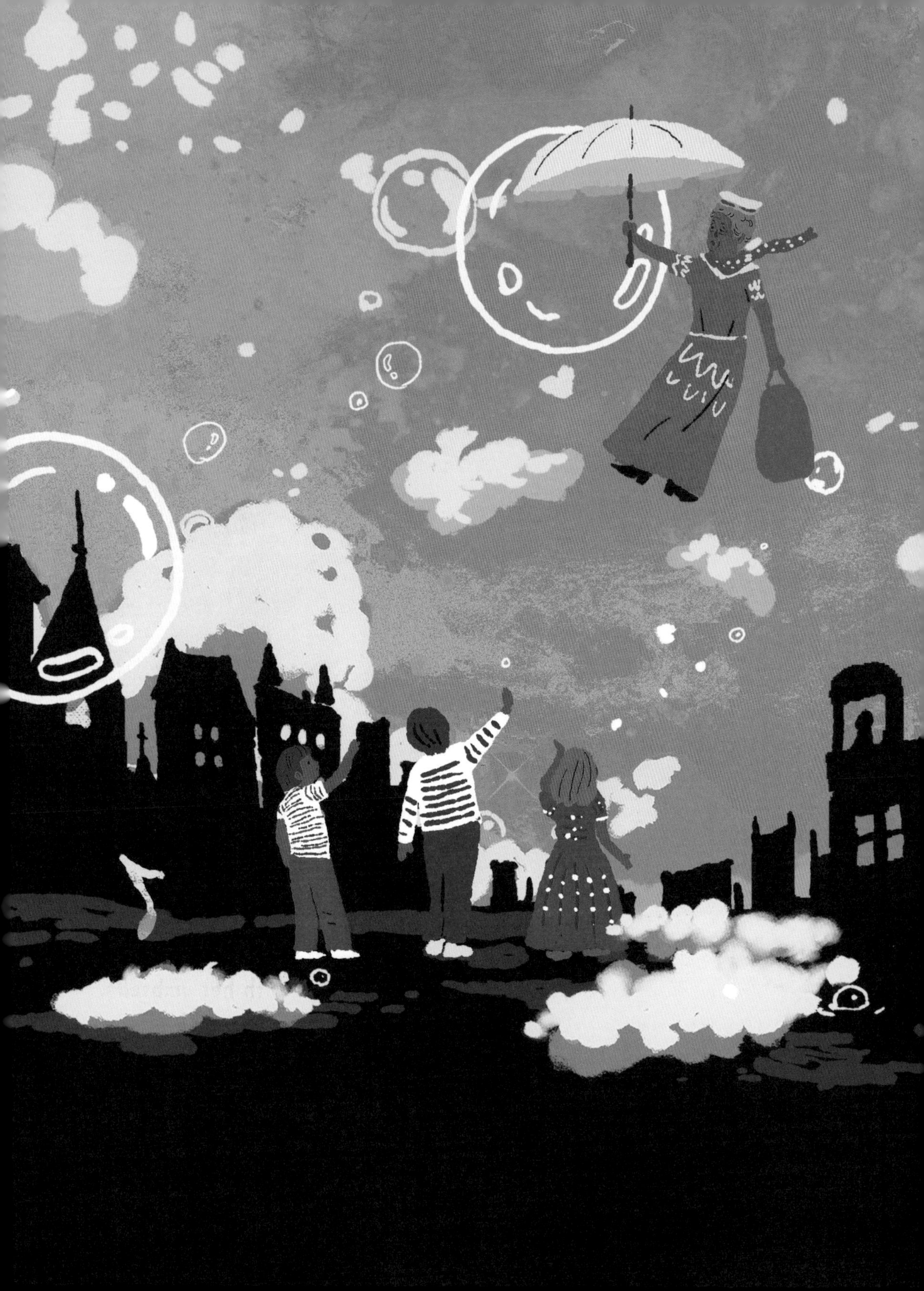

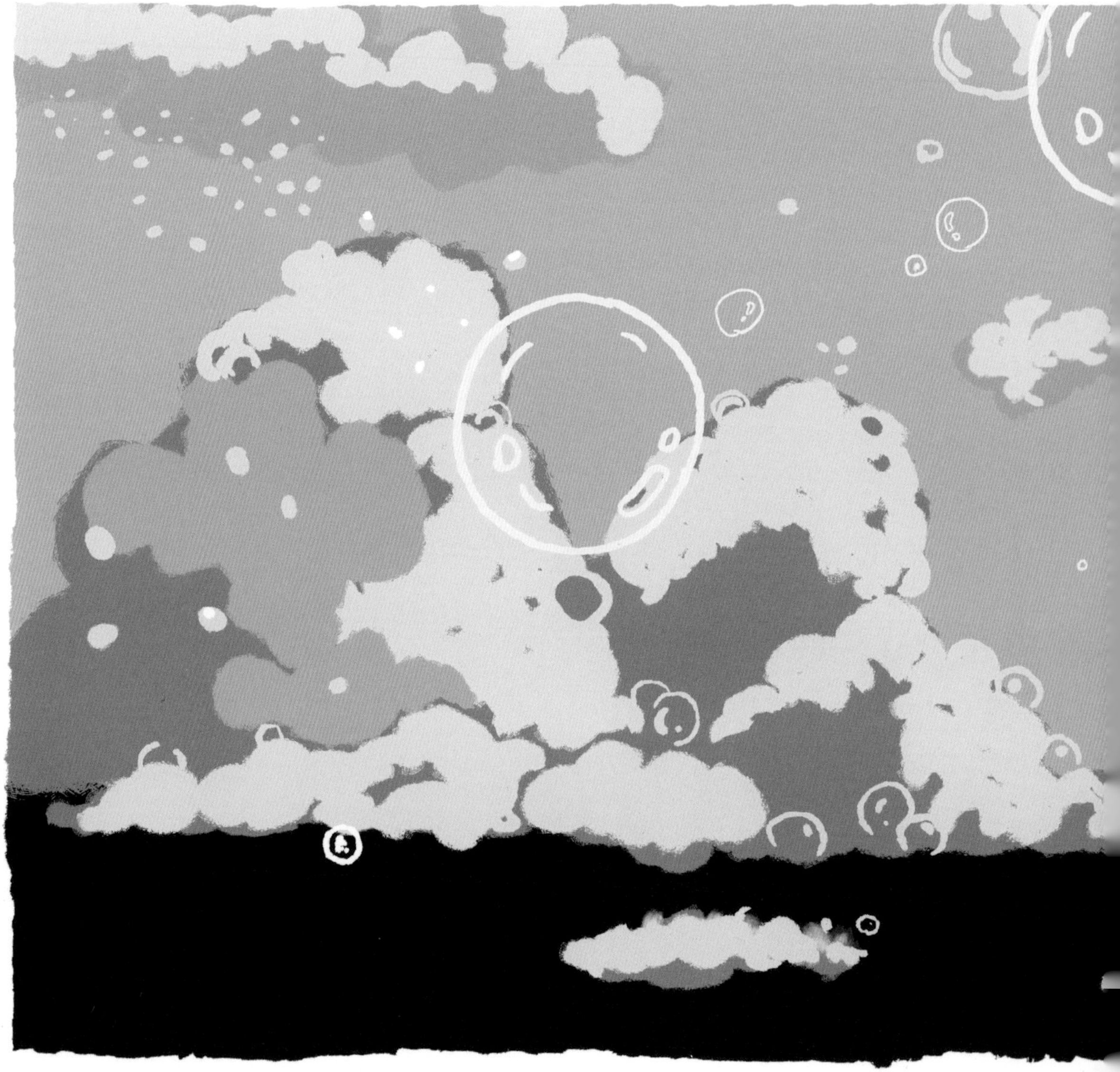

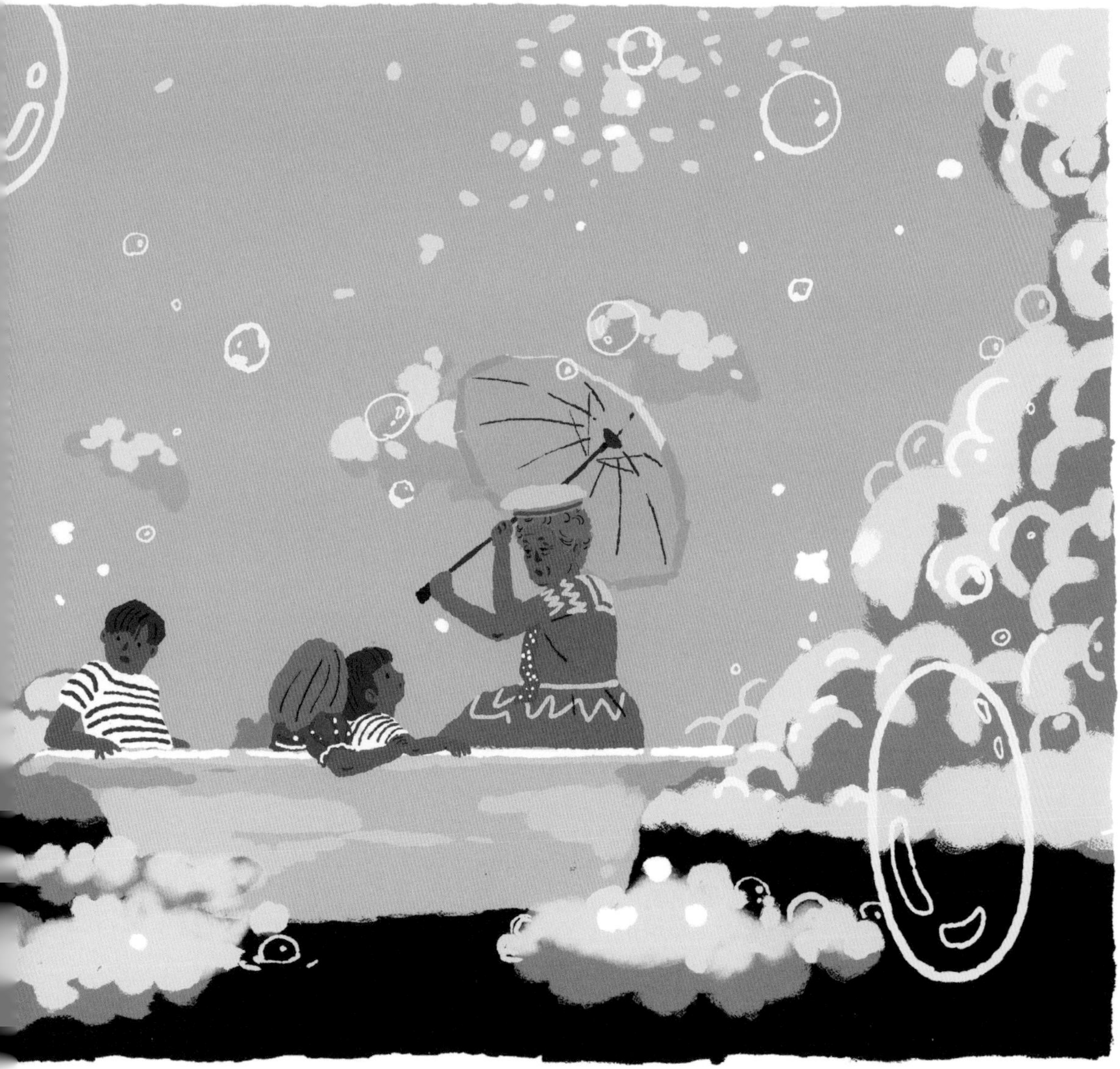

I hope that soon, for the Grandmothers and for us all,
peace and happiness will come, just like in this story.

The Grandmother Who Loved the Sea

Grandmother Choi Ok-ee

Grandmother was forced to Taiwan when she was 16.
She asked to be allowed to say goodbye to her parents
but they told her they would do it for her
and forced her along.

Grandmother Choi Ok-ee.

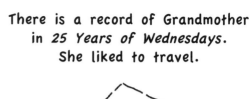

There is a record of Grandmother in *25 Years of Wednesdays*. She liked to travel.

Grandmother.... She had a lot of spirit so when music was played she would dance.

Swaying...

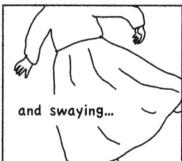

and swaying...

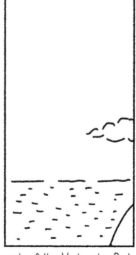

• A book that holds records of the Wednesday Protests in front of the Japanese embassy and of "comfort women." It informs people of past war crimes committed against these women and demands apologies by Japan. (Yoon Mi-Hyang, 2016).

We remember the hard life of Grandmother Choi Ok-ee.

Beautiful, Strong, and Grand

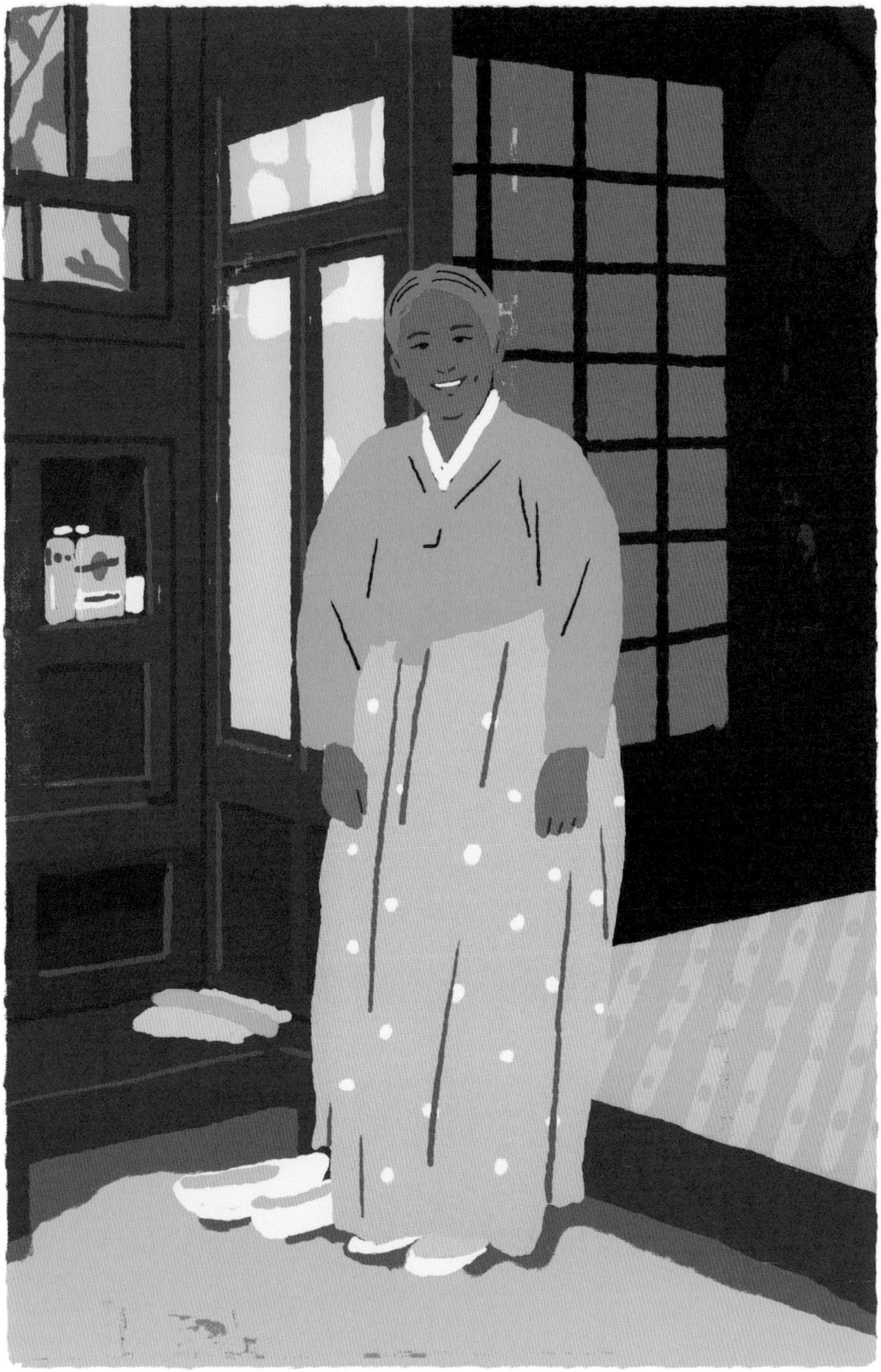

Lovely and Dainty Grandmother Han Ok-seon

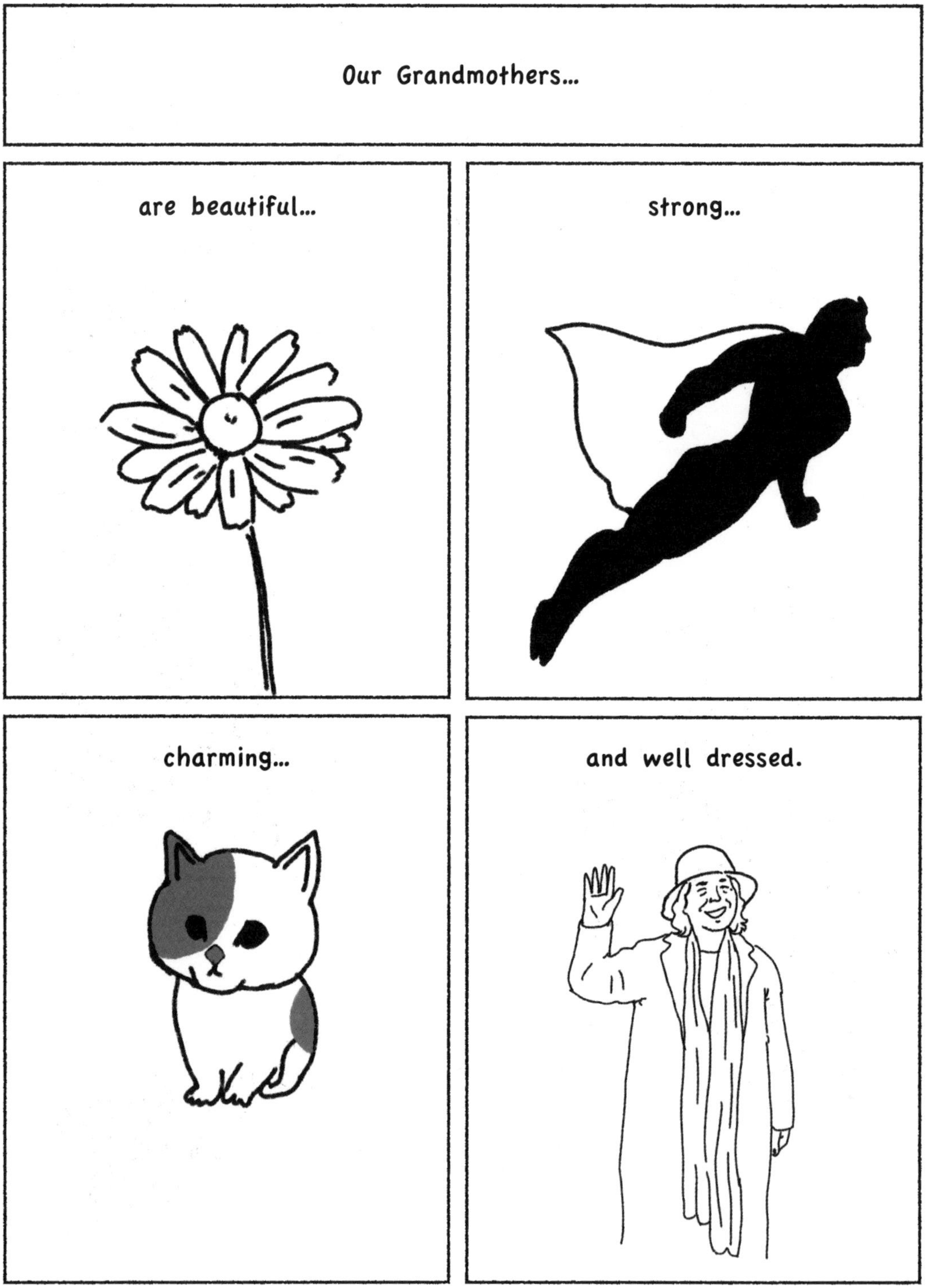
Our Grandmothers...
are beautiful...
strong...
charming...
and well dressed.

Some can sing with lovely voices...

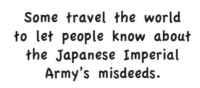

Some travel the world to let people know about the Japanese Imperial Army's misdeeds.

Sometimes they smile so lovingly...

and some shine like movie stars.

A Grandmother Riding the Subway

On a hot day in August, I came upon news that
our Grandmothers were leaving us one by one.
Now, there are barely 20 survivors.

On the subway, my eyes frequently met the eyes of a grandmother
who was gazing out the window at the river.
And I drew these pictures to make an animation.

I intended to put in the caption:
"Our Living Grandmothers as of August, 0000."

...But this work was discontinued....

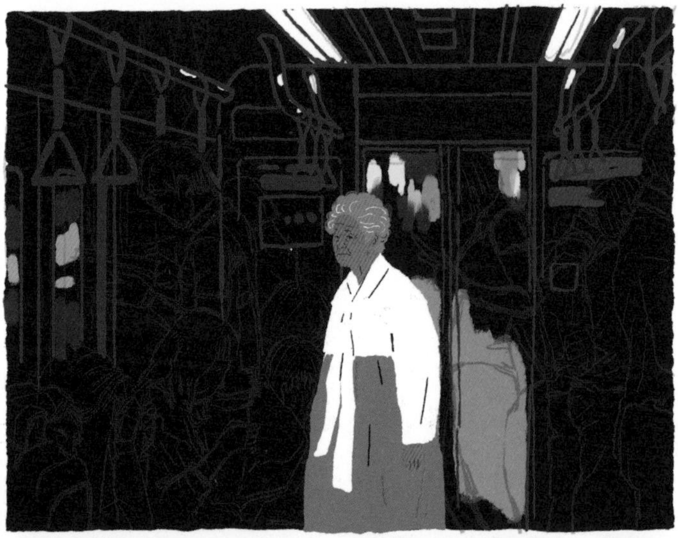

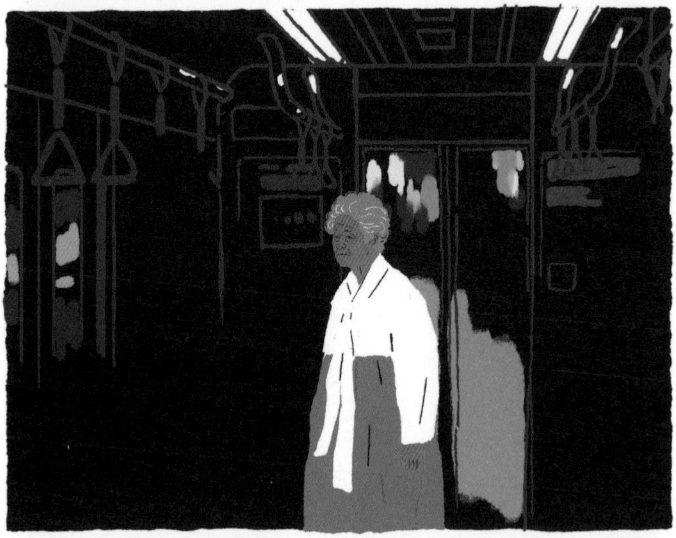

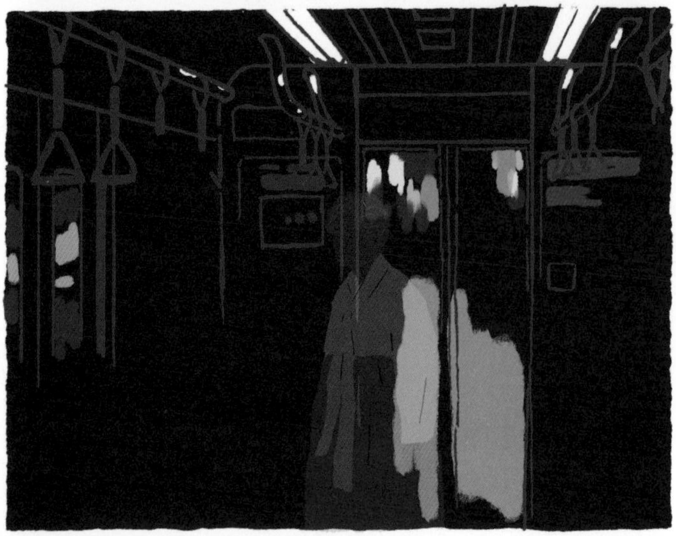

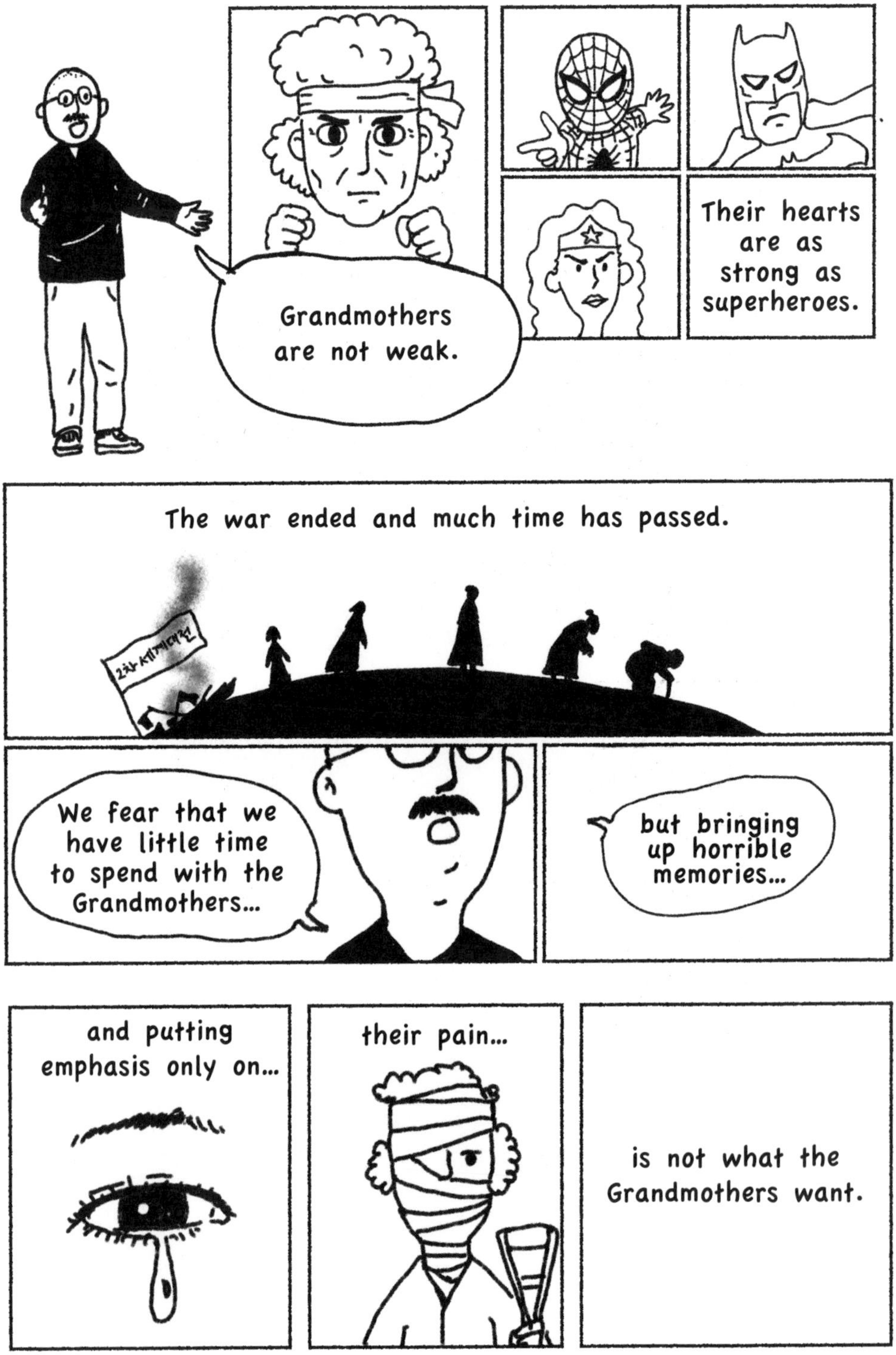
Grandmothers are not weak.
Their hearts are as strong as superheroes.
The war ended and much time has passed.
We fear that we have little time to spend with the Grandmothers...
but bringing up horrible memories...
and putting emphasis only on...
their pain...
is not what the Grandmothers want.

On a summer day in 2019, I read an article
that said a Grandmother felt so stressed whenever
the media mentioned the "number of survivors" that
her heart beat so fast she could not sleep from stress.

I felt so bad for her.

I was very ashamed that the terms, expressions
and actions we used to bring their situation to light
can actually cause fresh pain and
fresh wounds in the Grandmothers.

Whenever we talk of other people's pain,
we need to be very careful and
considerate of their feelings.

A Very Special Pitch and Hit

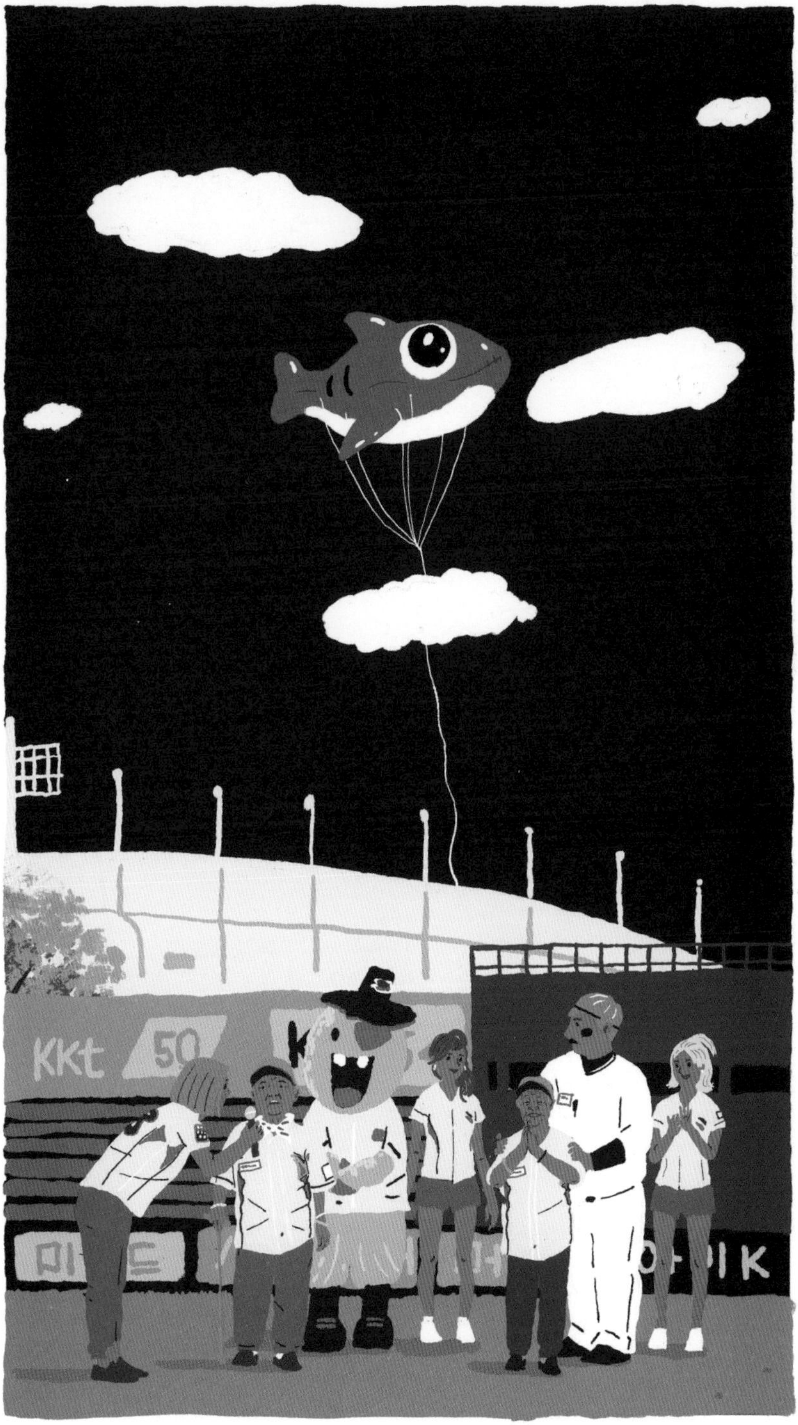
KKt
50

Grandmothers Who Play Baseball

Grandmother Lee Ok-seon

Grandmother Park Ok-seon

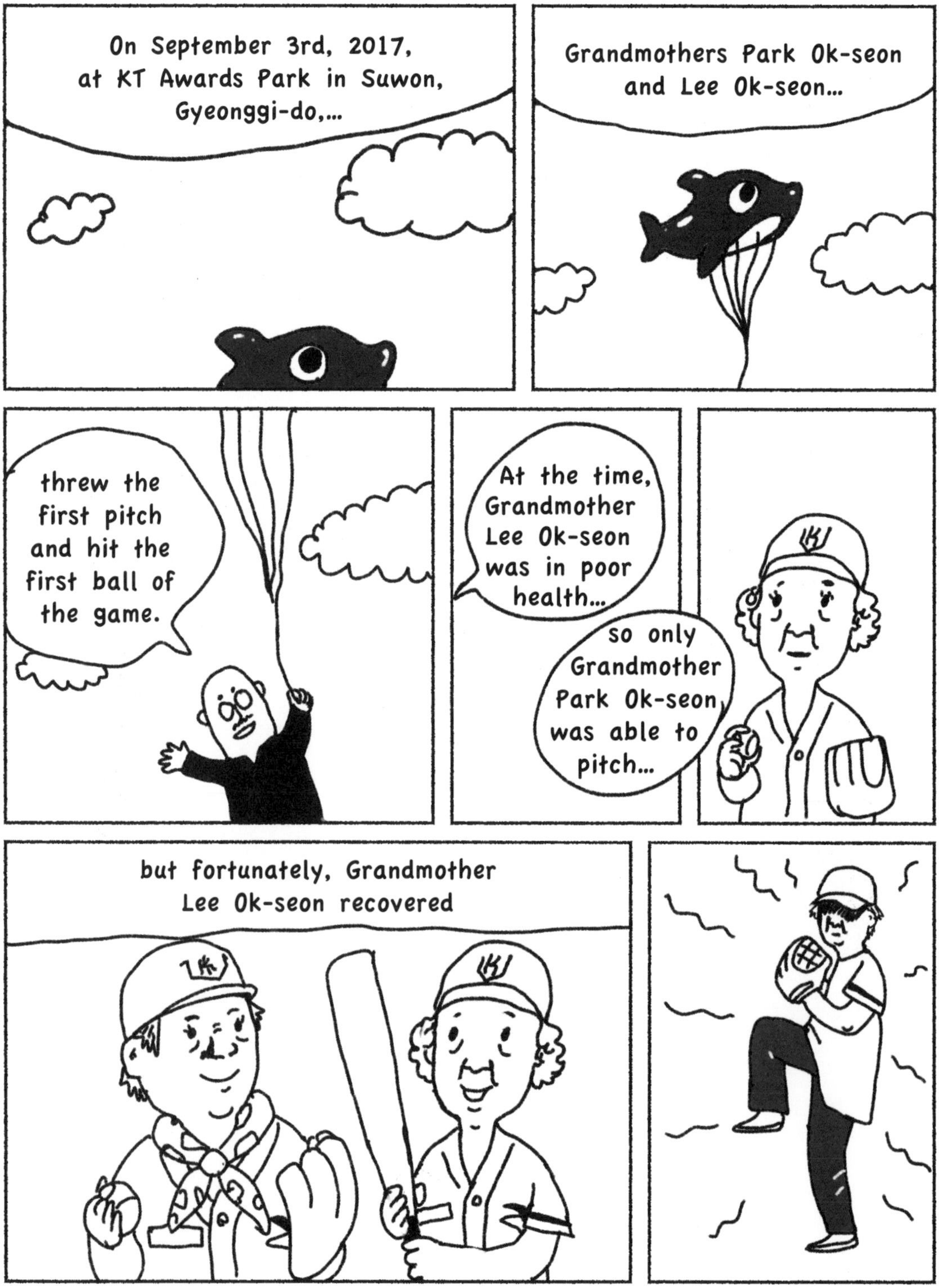
On September 3rd, 2017, at KT Awards Park in Suwon, Gyeonggi-do,...
Grandmothers Park Ok-seon and Lee Ok-seon...
threw the first pitch and hit the first ball of the game.
At the time, Grandmother Lee Ok-seon was in poor health...
so only Grandmother Park Ok-seon was able to pitch...
but fortunately, Grandmother Lee Ok-seon recovered

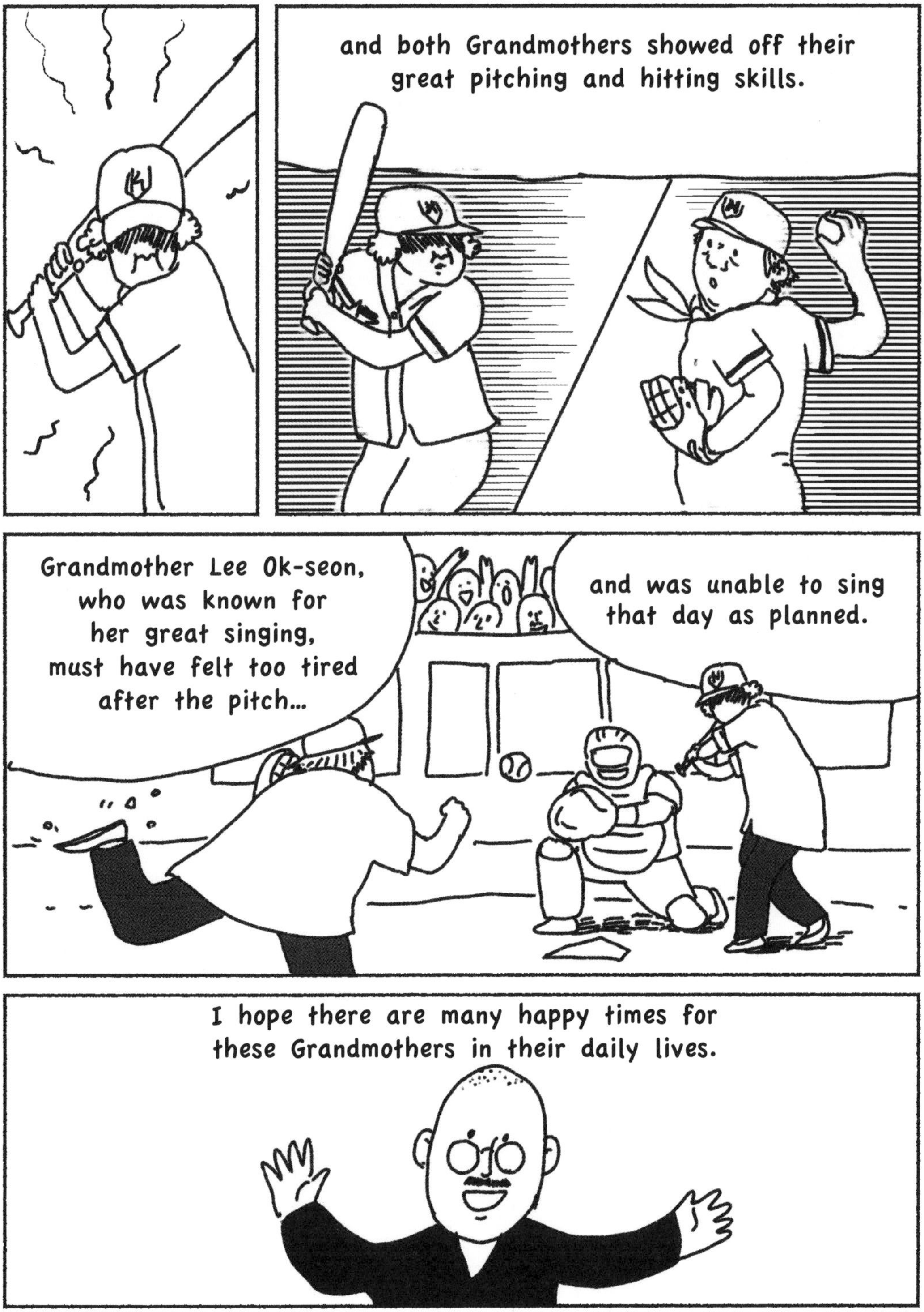

and both Grandmothers showed off their great pitching and hitting skills.
Grandmother Lee Ok-seon, who was known for her great singing, must have felt too tired after the pitch...
and was unable to sing that day as planned.
I hope there are many happy times for these Grandmothers in their daily lives.

People with Beautiful Minds

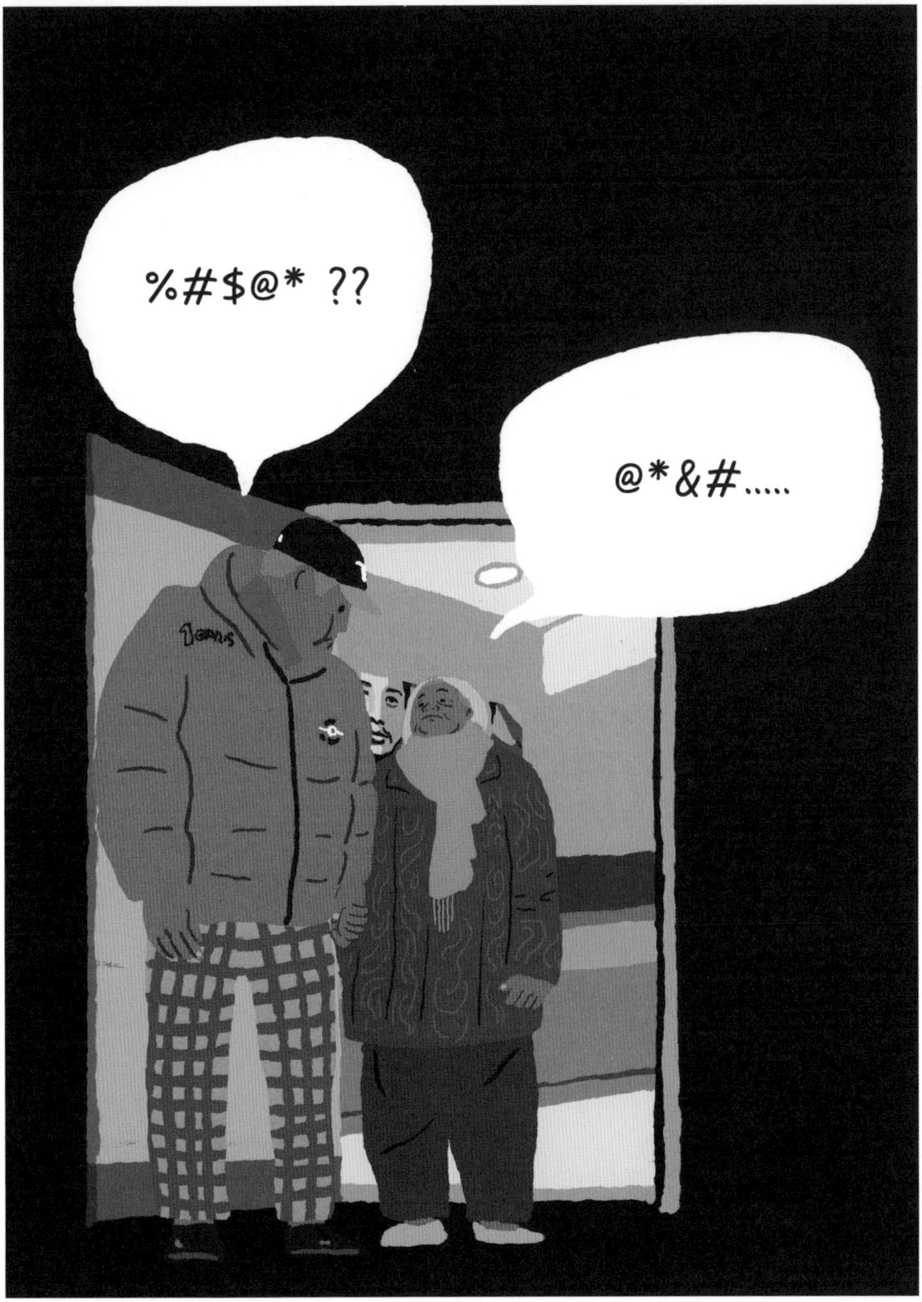
%#$@* ??
@*&#.....

On a cold winter day, Grandmother Park Ok-seon watched the musical, *Hero*, at the Seoul Arts Center with a television celebrity.

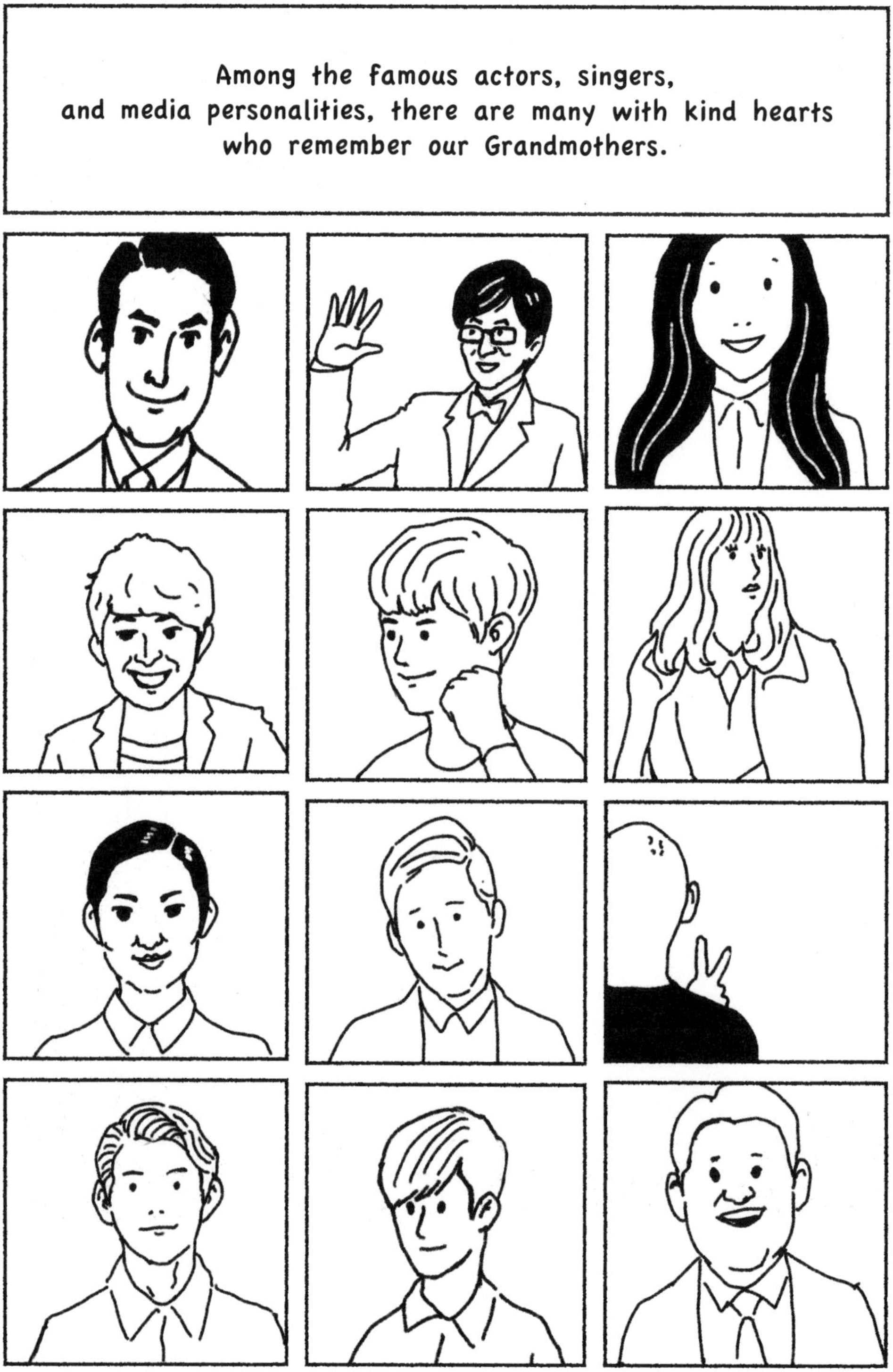
Among the famous actors, singers,
and media personalities, there are many with kind hearts
who remember our Grandmothers.

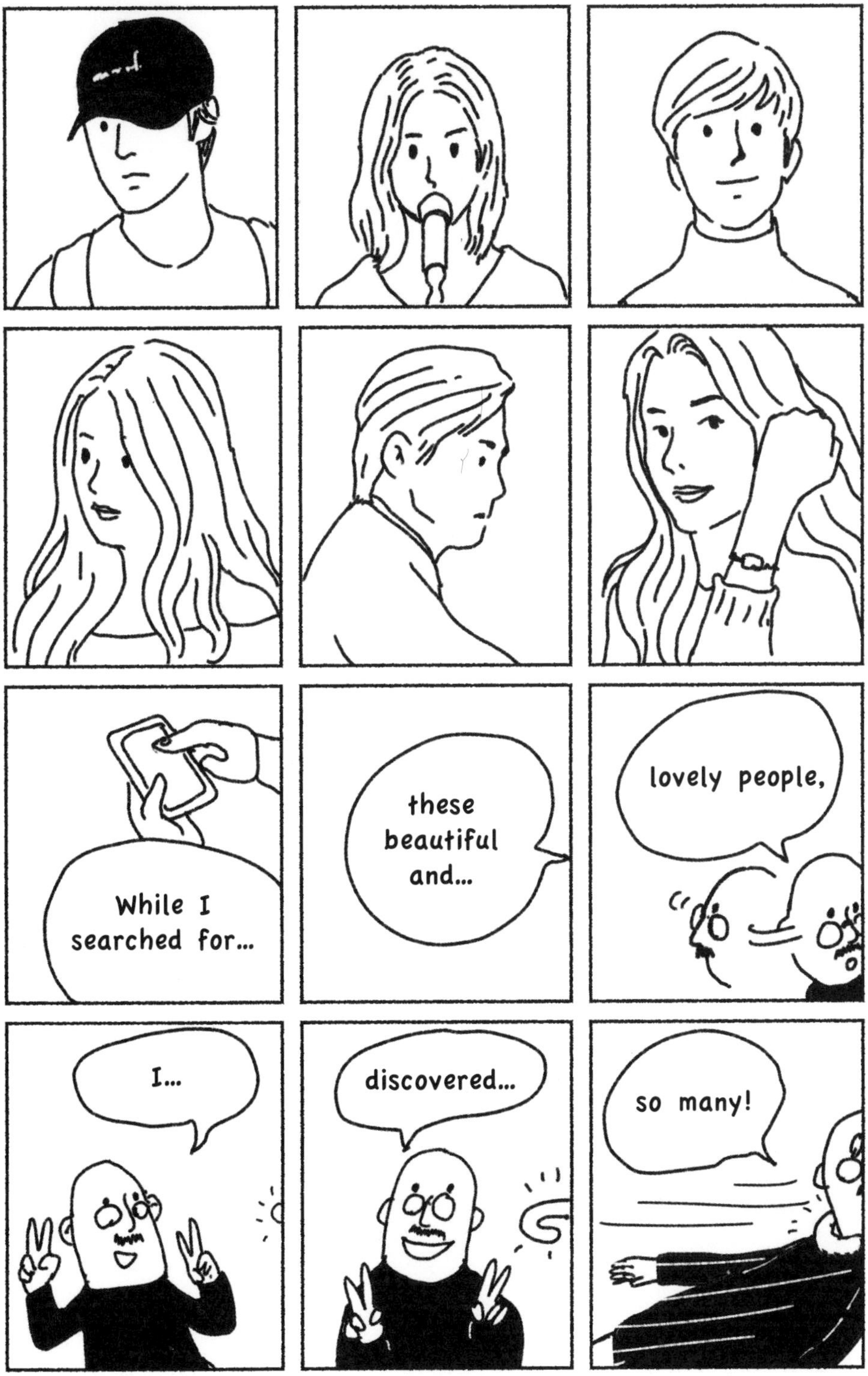
While I searched for...
these beautiful and...
lovely people,
I...
discovered...
so many!

We Will Not Forget!

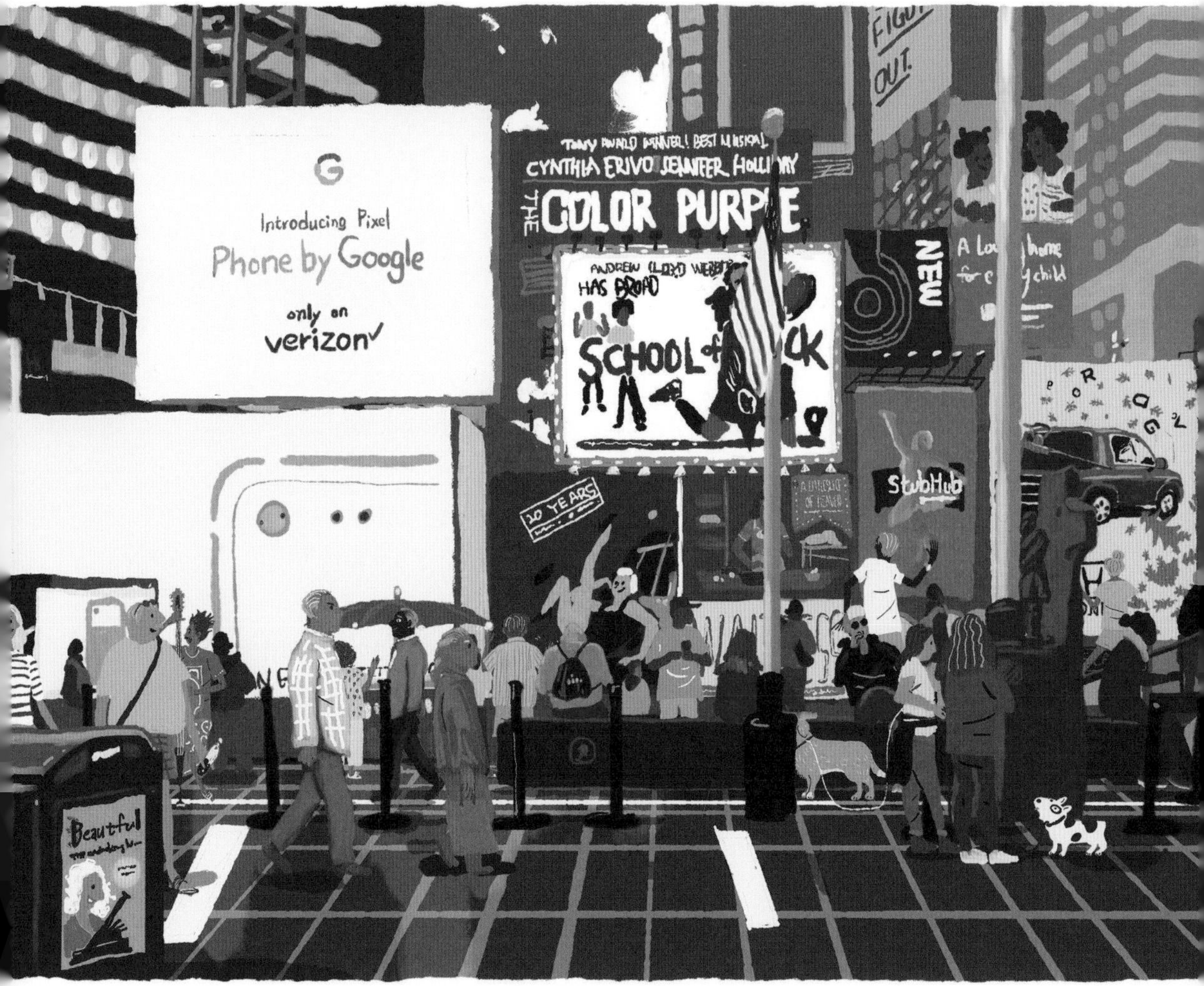
G
Introducing Pixel
Phone by Google
only on
verizon
CYNTHIA ERIVO
10 YEARS
StubHub
NEW
OUT.

Grandmothers in New York

I have this story in my head.

Grandmother visits Times Square in New York.
This place is always so dazzling and there are always lots of people.

She takes a photo with this dazzling background.

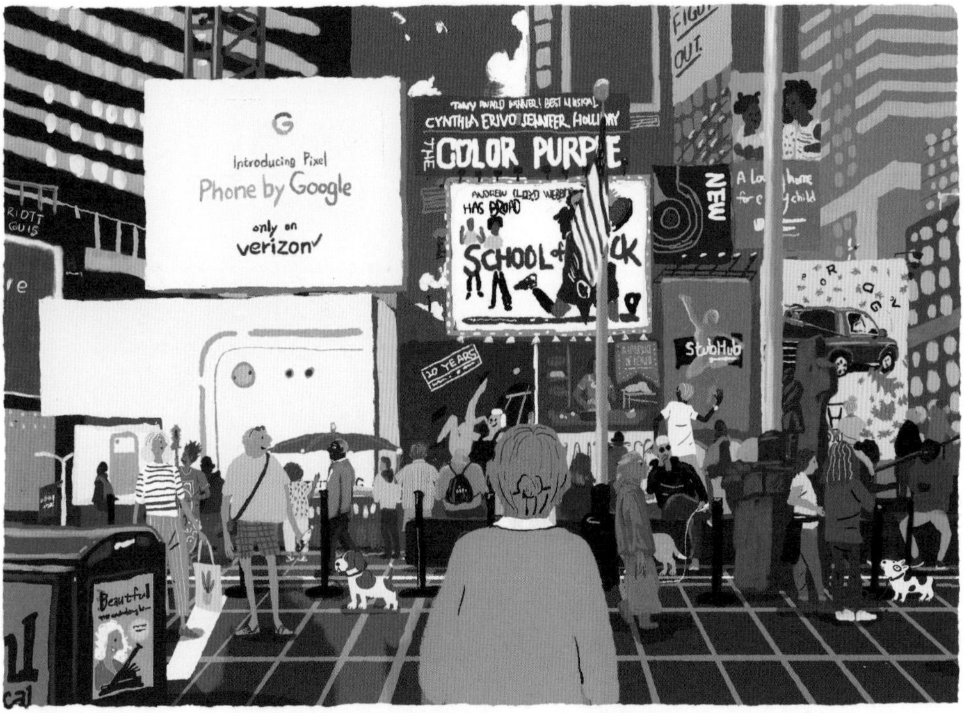
G
Introducing Pixel
Phone by Google
only on
verizon
CYNTHIA ERIVO JENNIFER HOLLIDAY
THE COLOR PURPLE
HAS BROAD
SCHOOL
NEW
StubHub
10 YEARS
Beautiful
OUT.

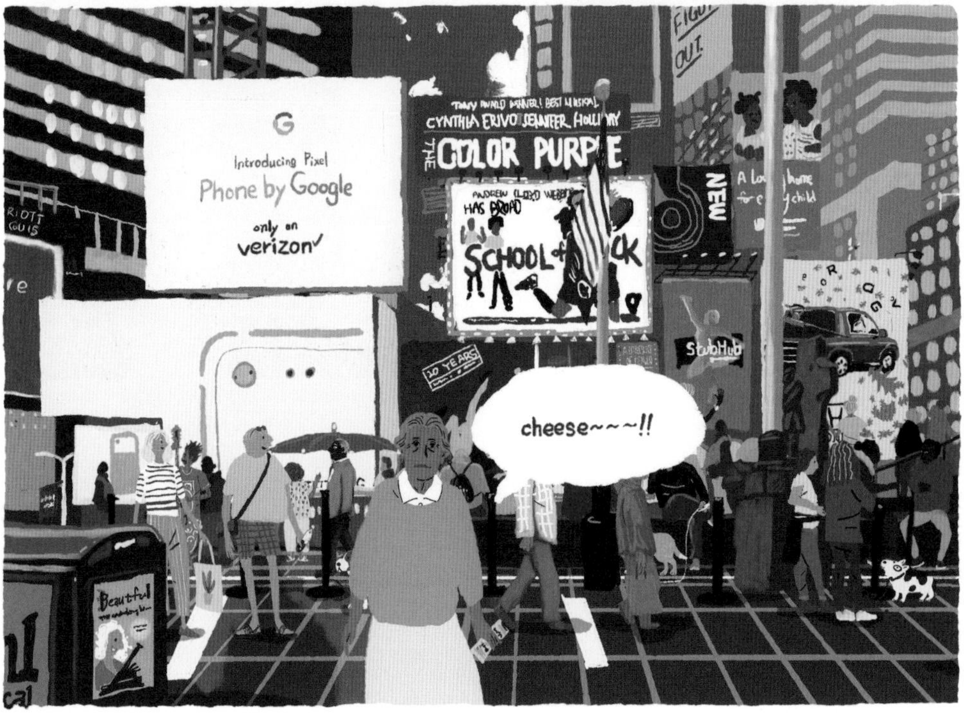
G
Introducing Pixel
Phone by Google
only on
verizon
CYNTHIA ERIVO JENNIFER HOLLIDAY
THE COLOR PURPLE
HAS BROAD
SCHOOL
NEW
StubHub
10 YEARS
Beautiful
OUT.
cheese~~~!!

One photo here...

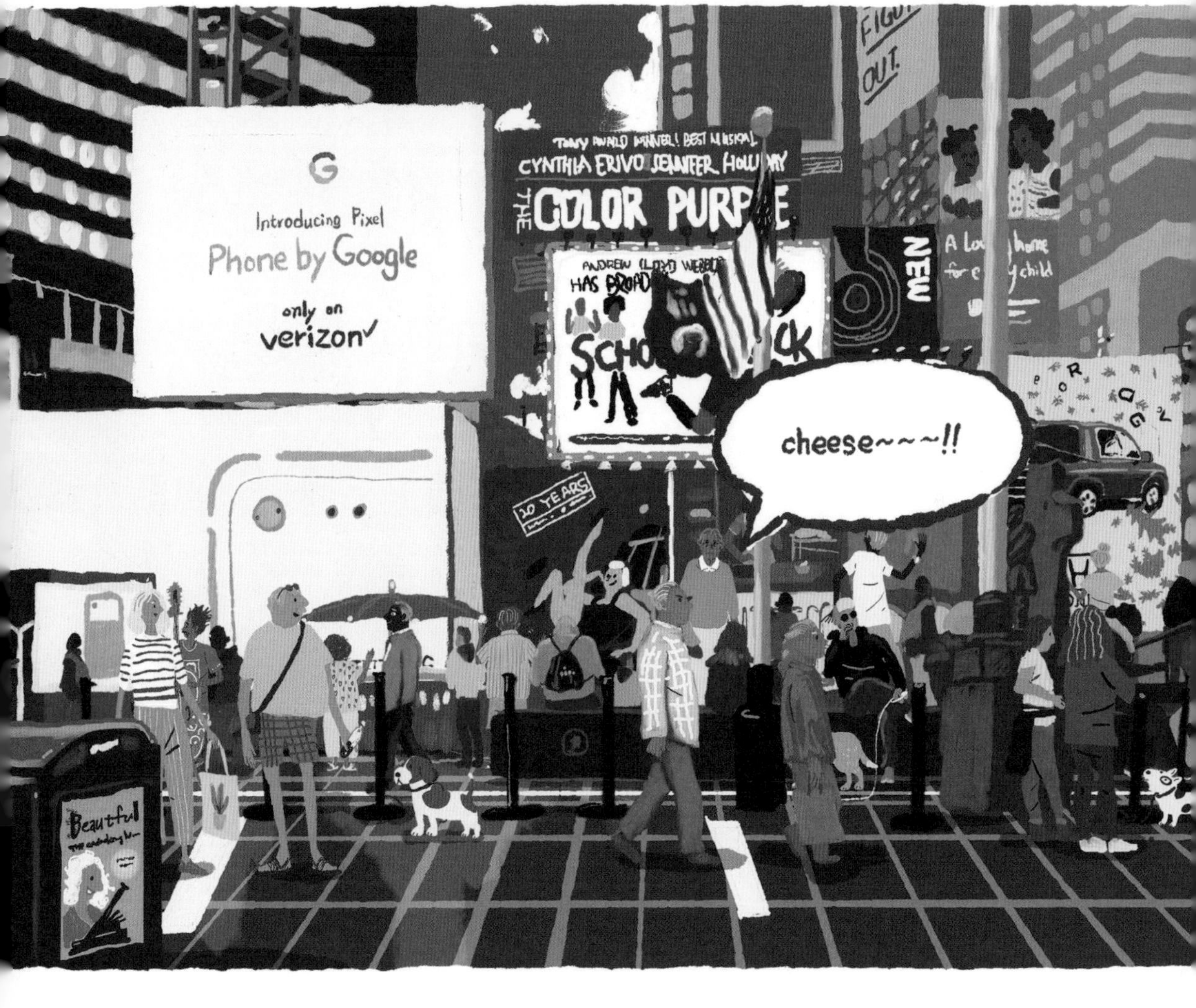
G
Introducing Pixel
Phone by Google
only on
verizon✓
20 YEARS
NEW
cheese~~~!!
Beautiful

and there.

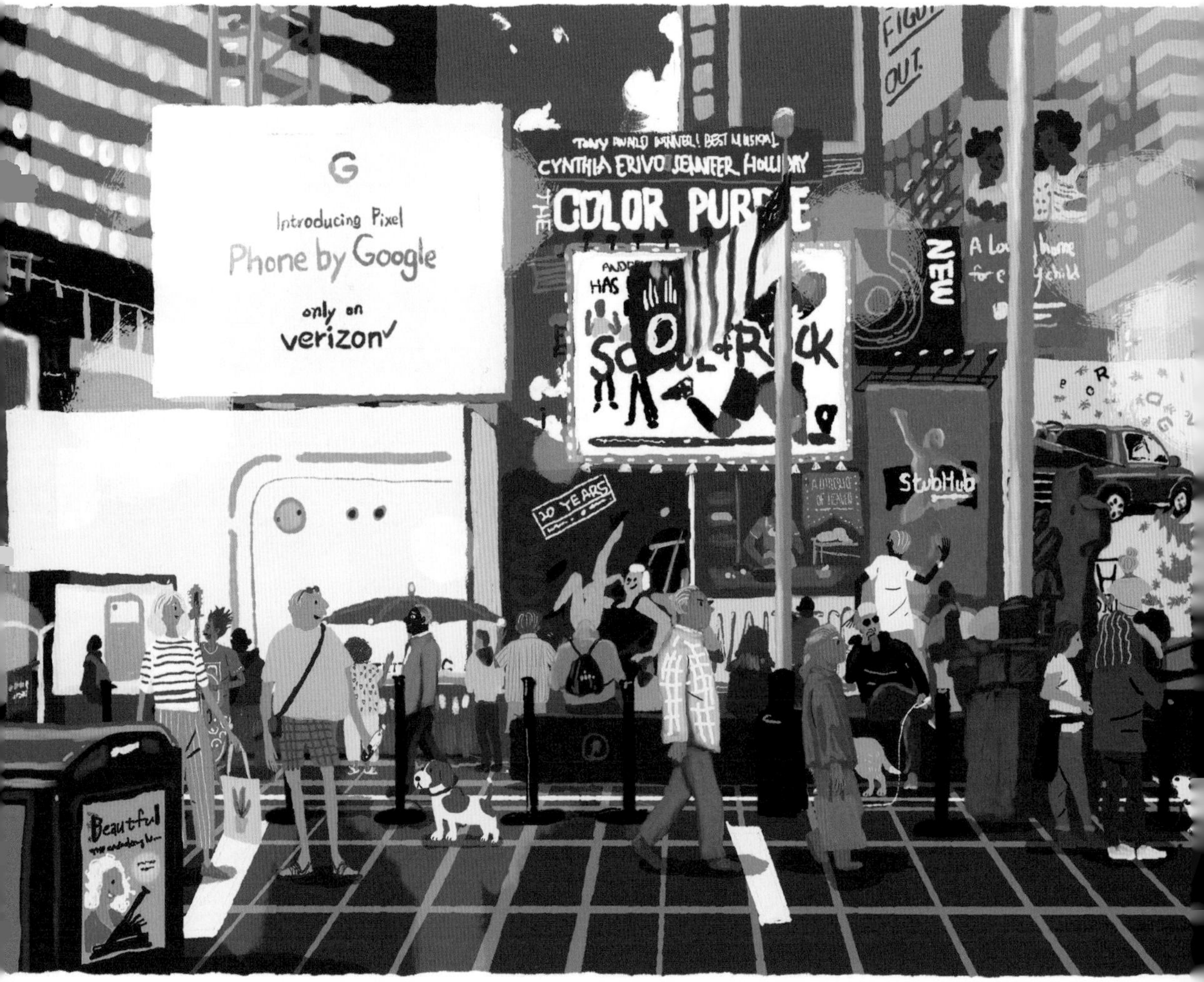
G
Introducing Pixel
Phone by Google
only on
verizon
CYNTHIA ERIVO JENNIFER HOLLIDAY
THE COLOR PURPLE
NEW
StubHub
20 YEARS
Beautiful

Times Square is filled with electric billboards.
It is dizzying but also beautiful.
We can see Samsung, LG, musical promotions...

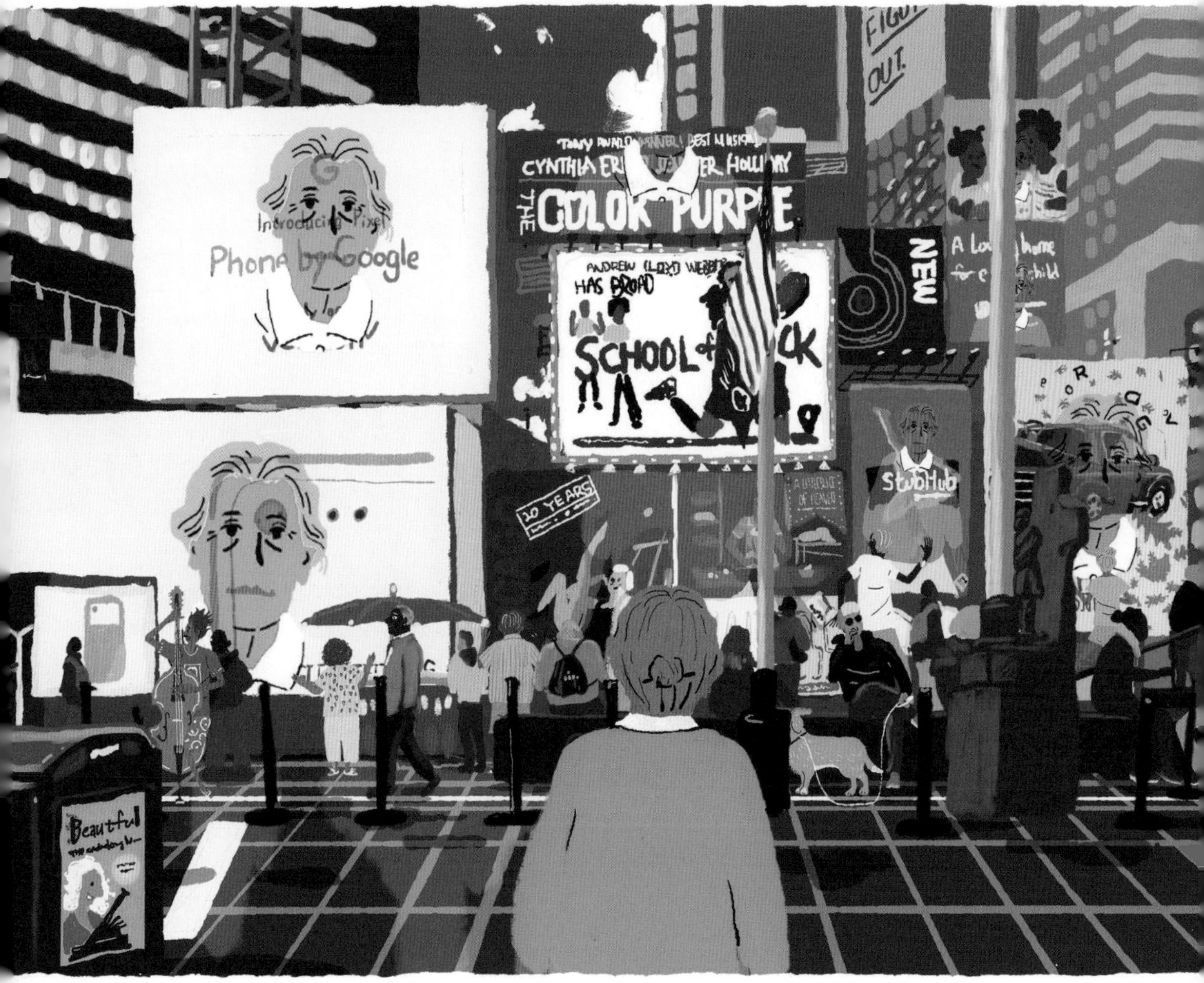
Phone by Google
THE COLOR PURPLE
NEW
StubHub
20 YEARS
Beautiful

Looking at the digital billboard...

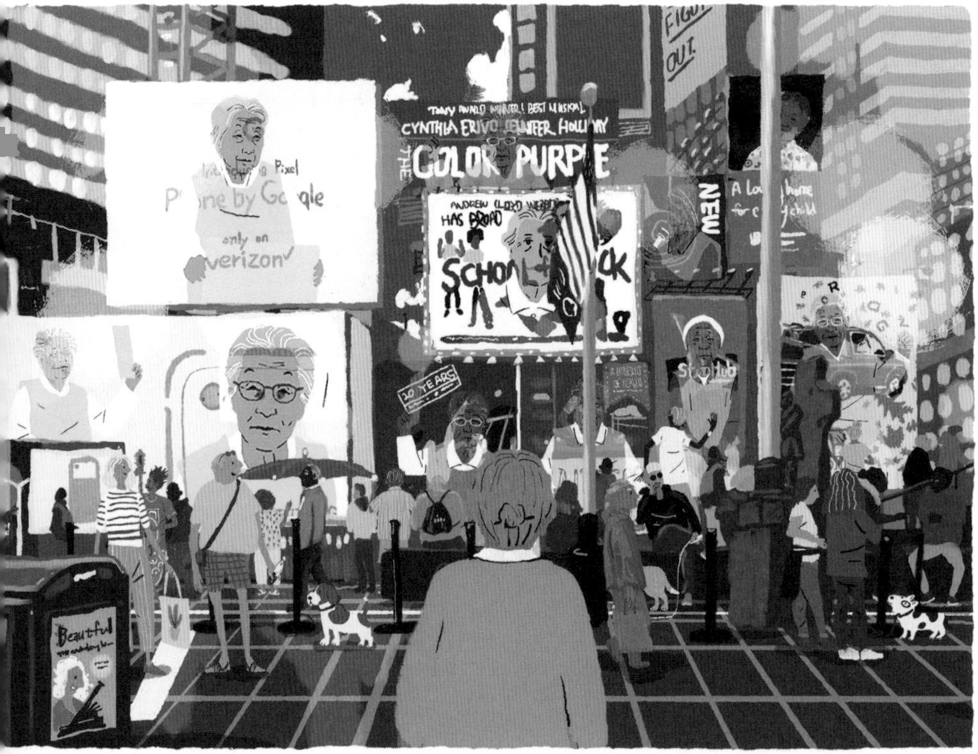
only on
verizon
NEW
20 YEARS
Beautiful

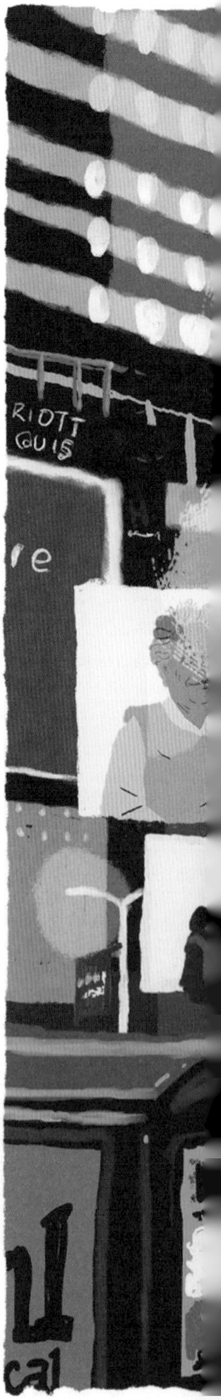

I imagine how good it would be to see the Grandmothers there. I wish each of their names would be called one by one.

Our Grandmothers will be remembered for a long time.

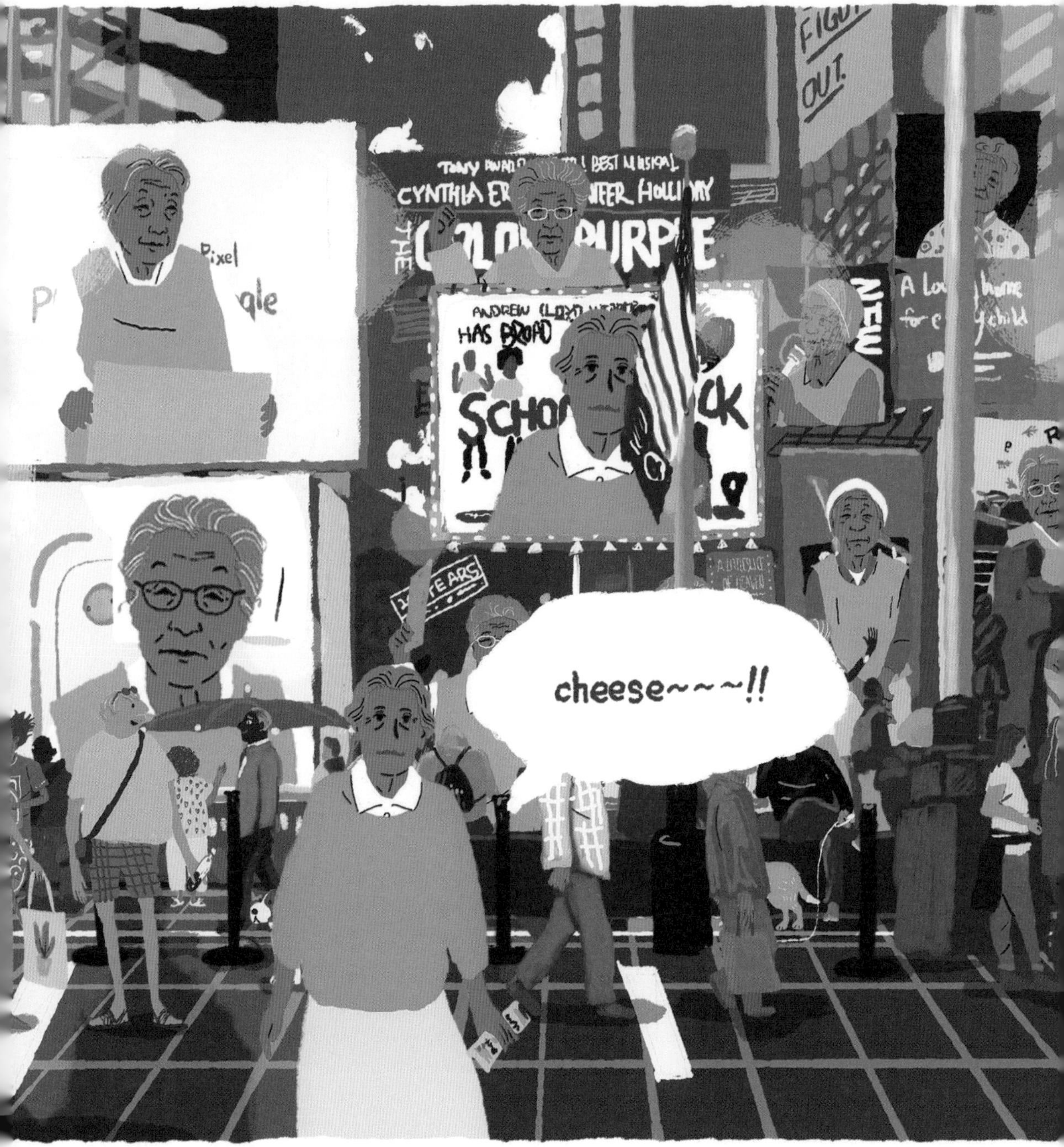
NEW
cheese~~~!!

CHAPTER 3

Traveling Together

Just 80 Years Ago...

Paris is a truly wonderful city.
It is filled with old buildings, roads, and subtle store signs.
It is truly extraordinary.
The city does not destroy things that are old.

The Eiffel Tower that Parisians thought so ugly was built in 1889.
This city where distant history, architecture, and art work still flow
is breathtaking. While walking by a building in Paris
I find myself remembering our Grandmothers.

When I look at these old buildings as I walk,
I naturally think about the pain
the Grandmothers felt 80 years ago.

Some people say we should forget the past.
That we cannot move forward if we stay in the past.

But how can we forget something that happened a mere 80 years ago?

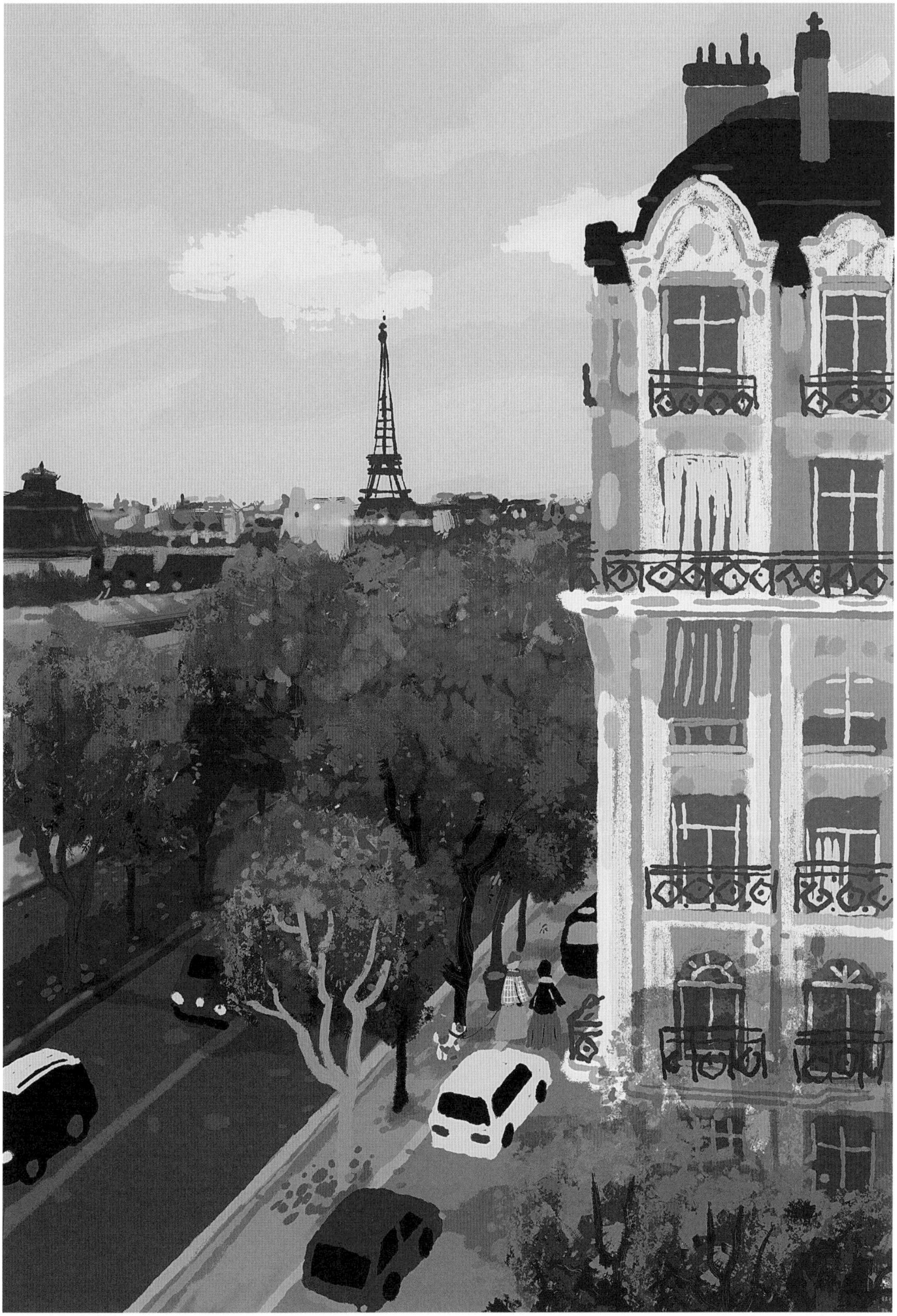

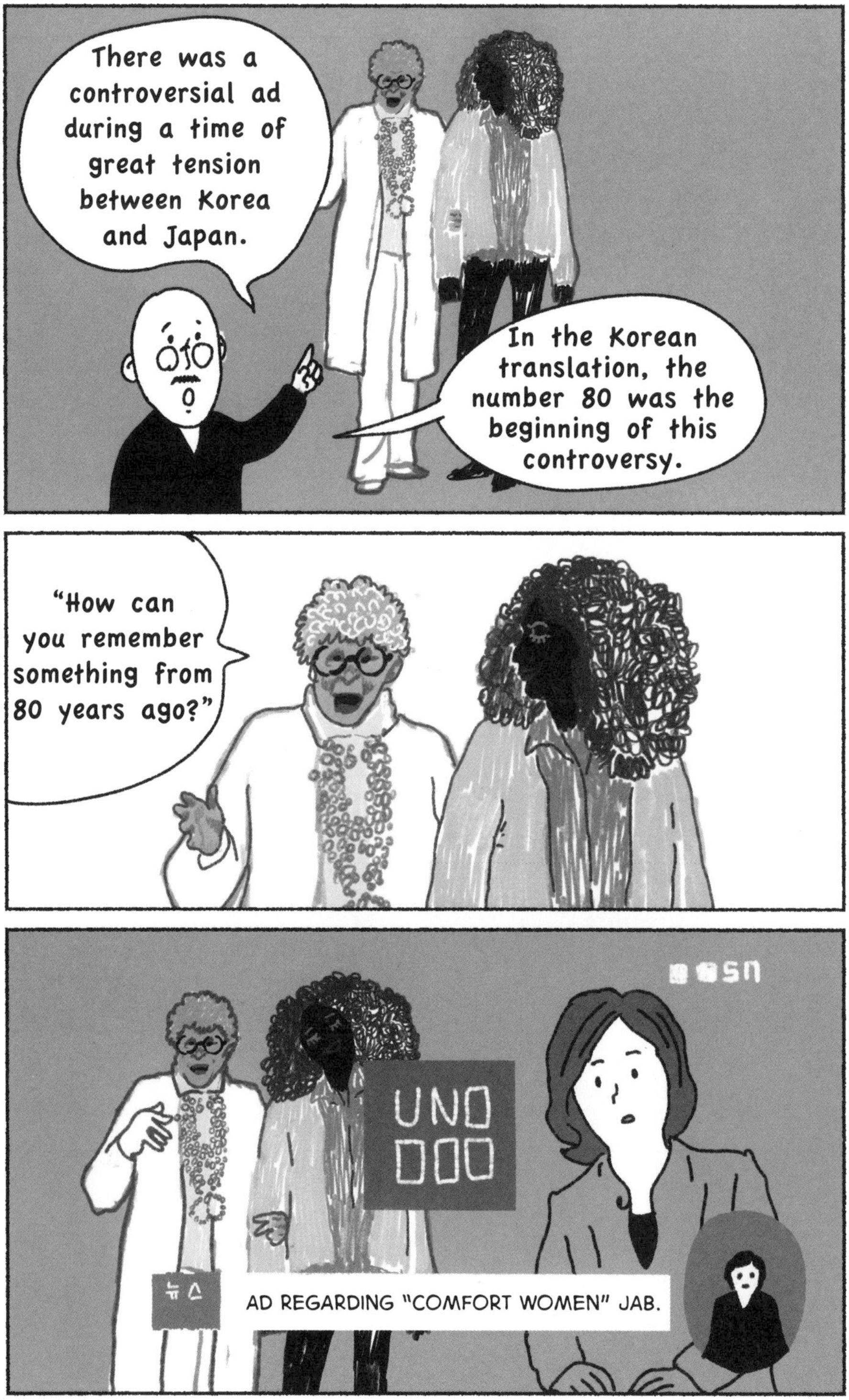
There was a controversial ad during a time of great tension between Korea and Japan.
In the Korean translation, the number 80 was the beginning of this controversy.
"How can you remember something from 80 years ago?"
뉴스
AD REGARDING "COMFORT WOMEN" JAB.

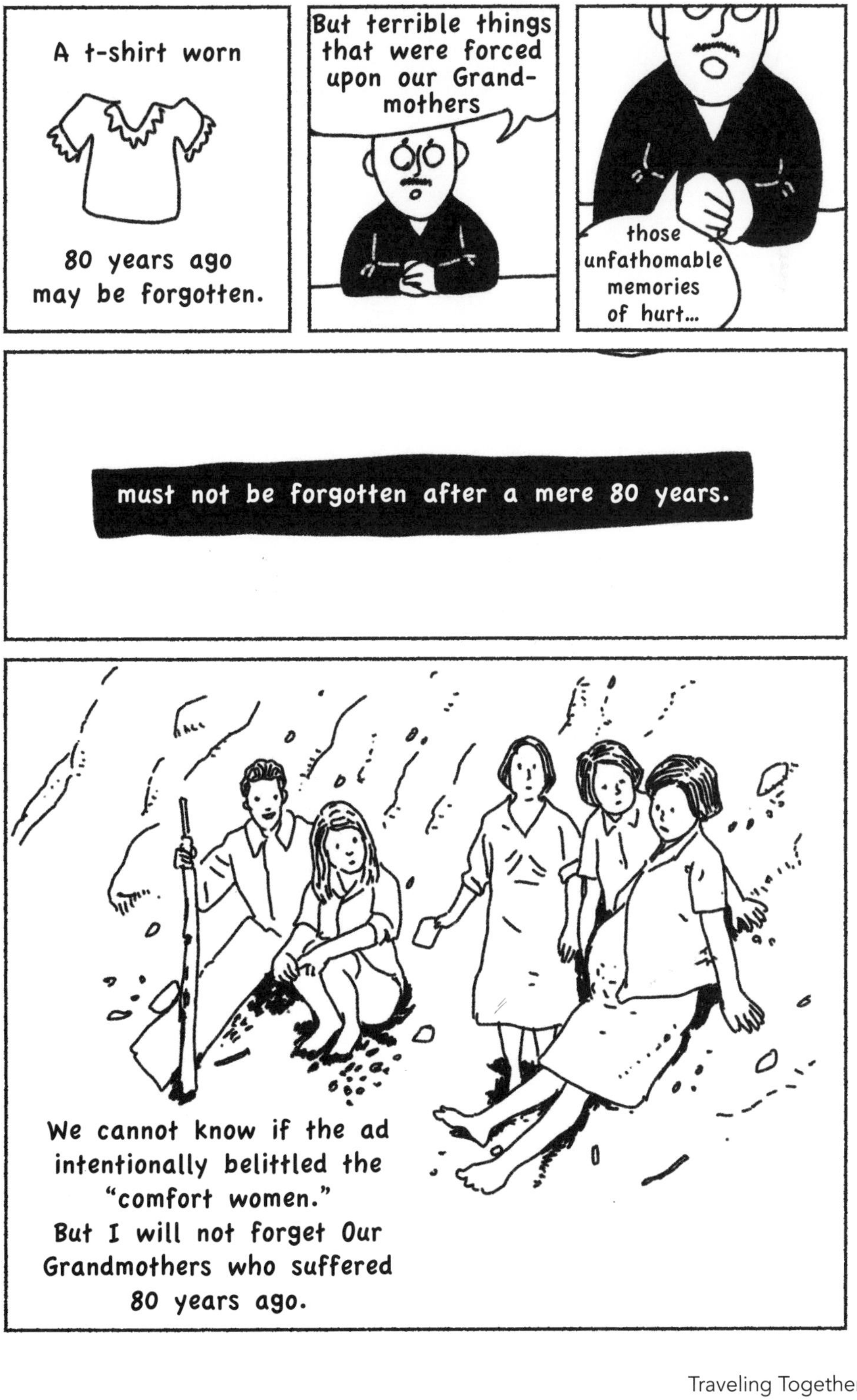
A t-shirt worn
80 years ago
may be forgotten.
But terrible things that were forced upon our Grand-mothers
those unfathomable memories of hurt...
must not be forgotten after a mere 80 years.
We cannot know if the ad intentionally belittled the "comfort women."
But I will not forget Our Grandmothers who suffered 80 years ago.

Don't Think You Are Alone

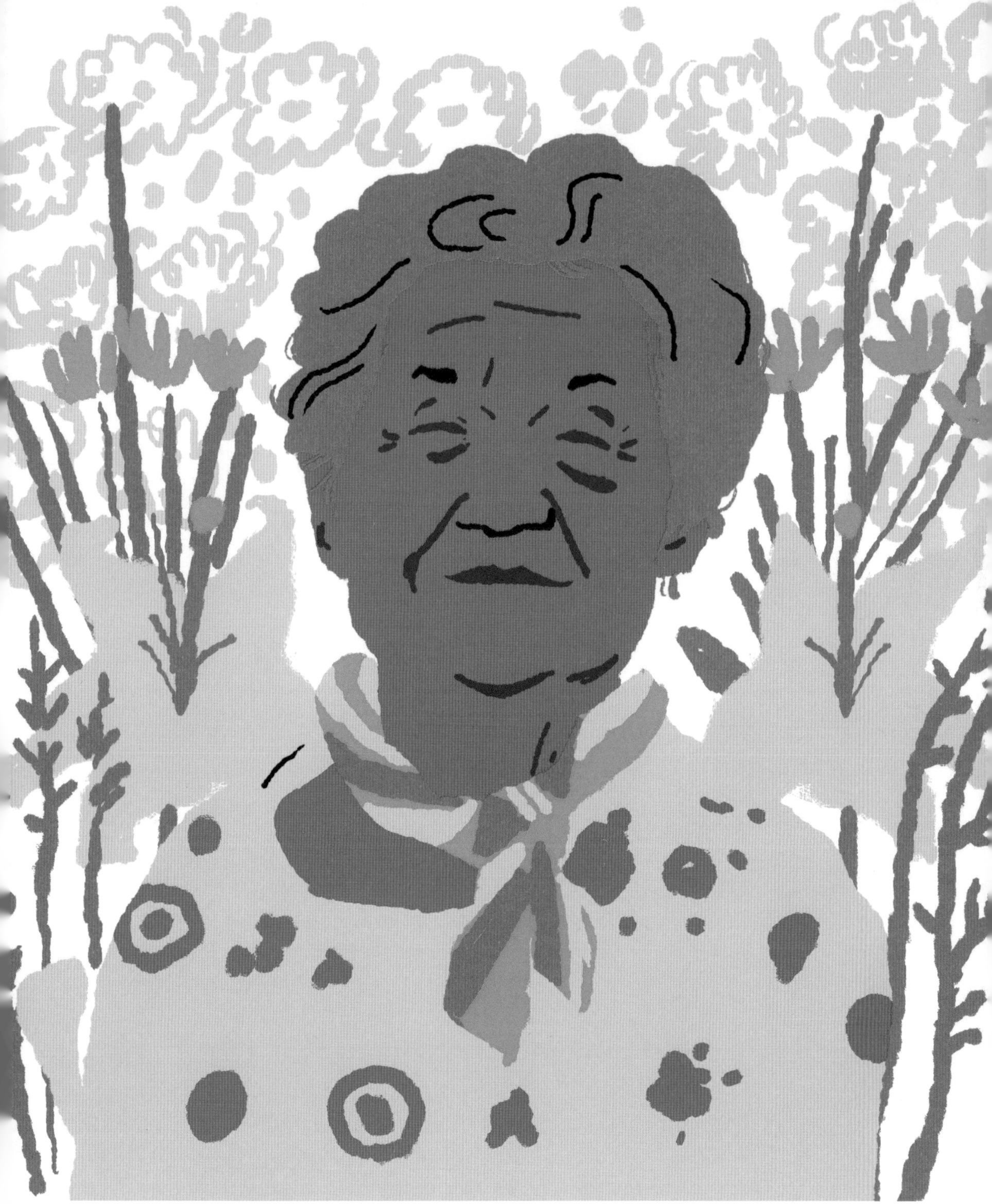

Grandmother Kim Gun-ja who stood by students

Grandmother Kim Gun-ja is the actual model for Okbum in the movie *I Can Speak*.

Grandmother Kim Gun-ja along with Grandmother Lee Yong-soo, and Jan Ruff O'Herne gave testimony about their victimization as "comfort women" by the Japanese Imperial Army at a US Congressional Hearing.

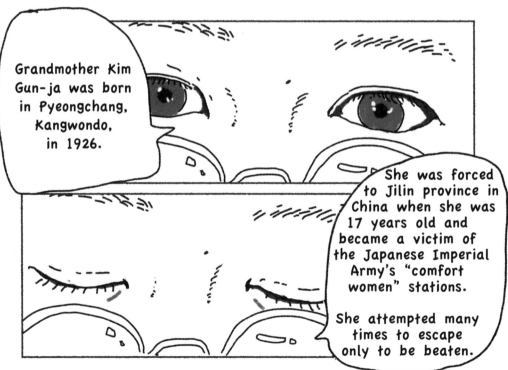

Grandmother Kim Gun-ja was born in Pyeongchang, Kangwondo, in 1926.

She was forced to Jilin province in China when she was 17 years old and became a victim of the Japanese Imperial Army's "comfort women" stations.

She attempted many times to escape only to be beaten.

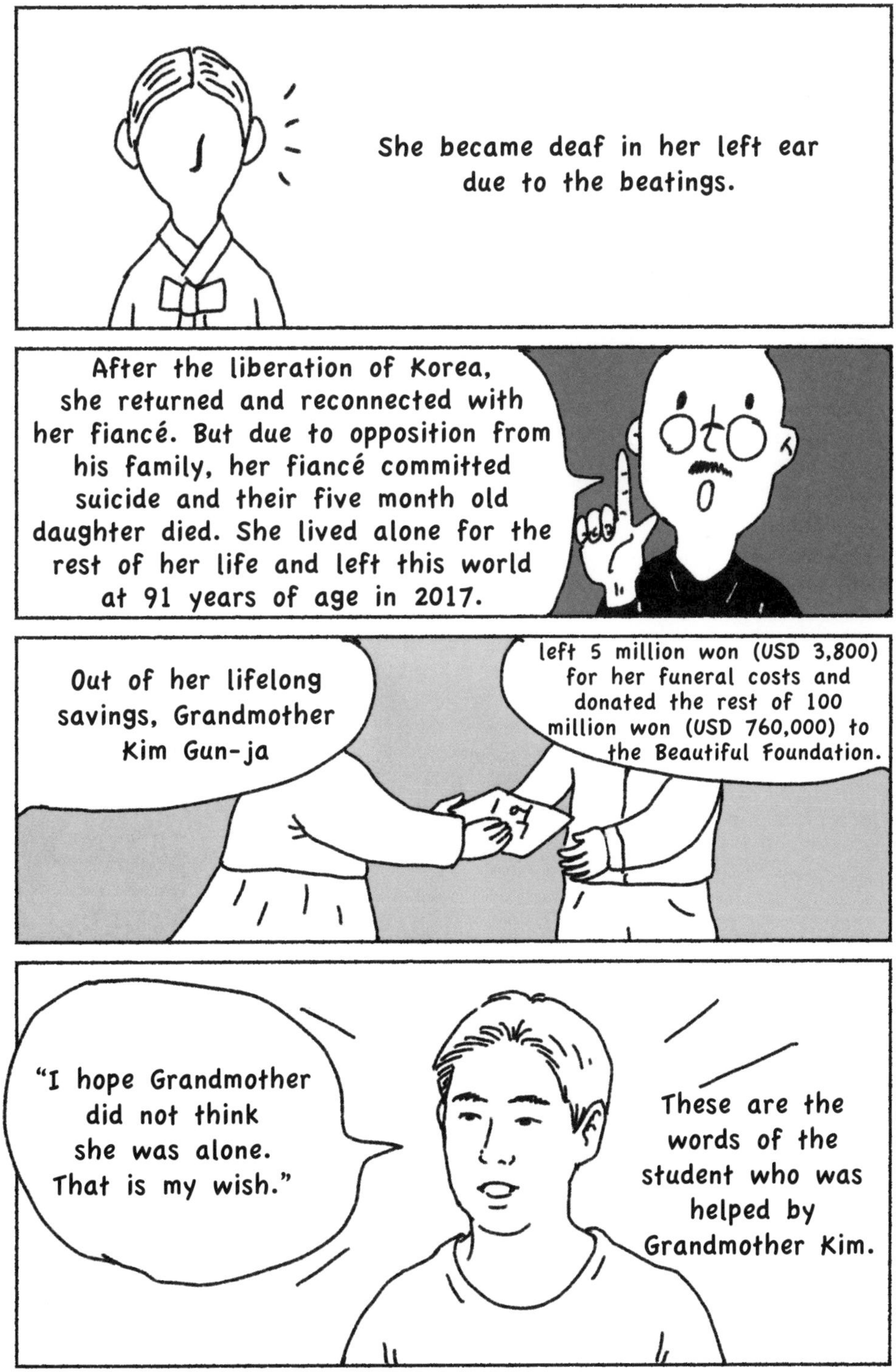
She became deaf in her left ear due to the beatings.
After the liberation of Korea, she returned and reconnected with her fiancé. But due to opposition from his family, her fiancé committed suicide and their five month old daughter died. She lived alone for the rest of her life and left this world at 91 years of age in 2017.
Out of her lifelong savings, Grandmother Kim Gun-ja
left 5 million won (USD 3,800) for her funeral costs and donated the rest of 100 million won (USD 760,000) to the Beautiful Foundation.
"I hope Grandmother did not think she was alone. That is my wish."
These are the words of the student who was helped by Grandmother Kim.

There Is Something I Have to Say

Grandmother Lee Yong-soo

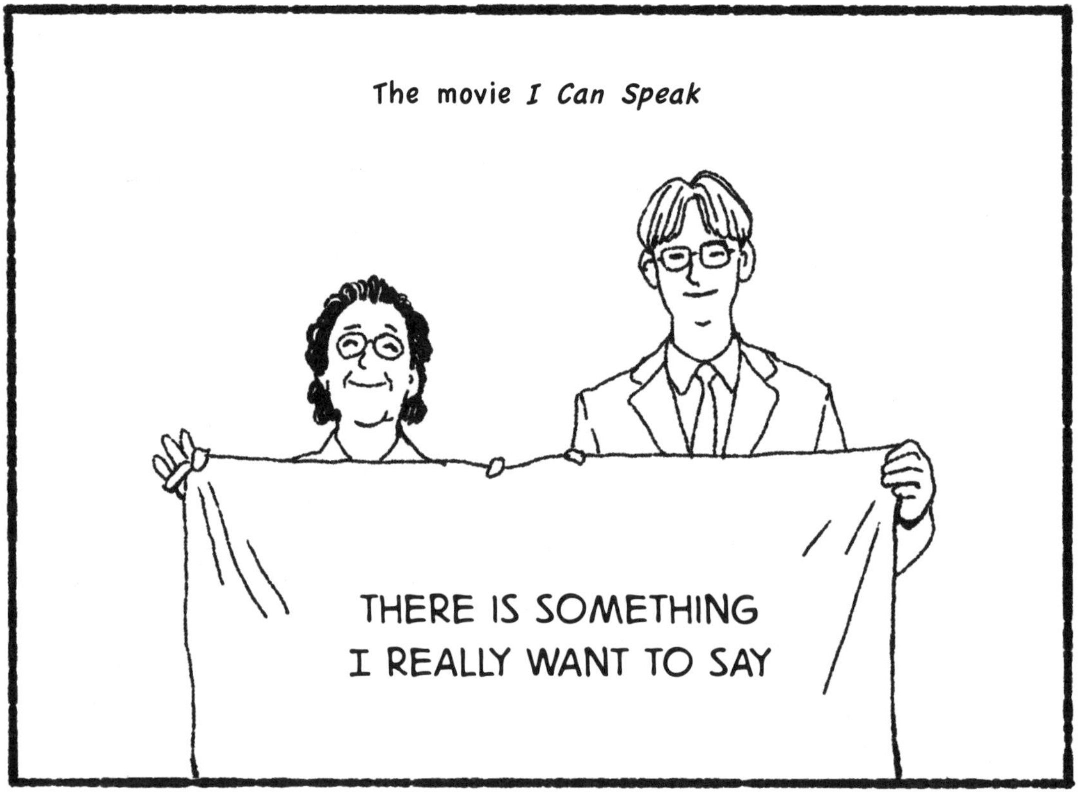
The movie *I Can Speak*
THERE IS SOMETHING I REALLY WANT TO SAY

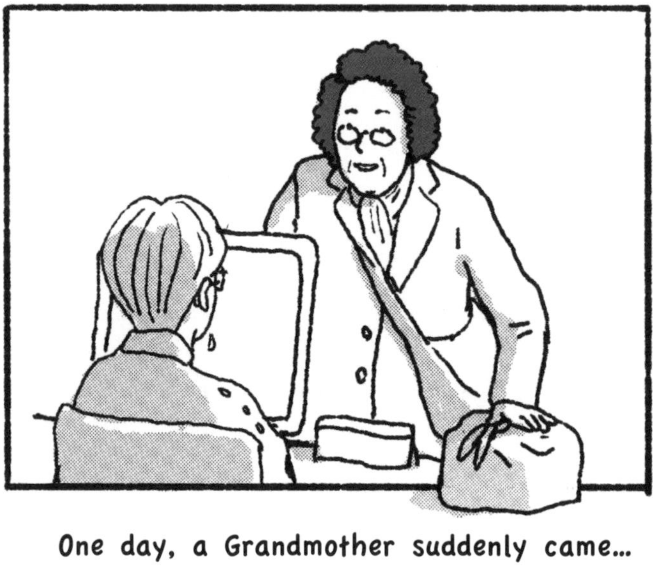

One day, a Grandmother suddenly came...

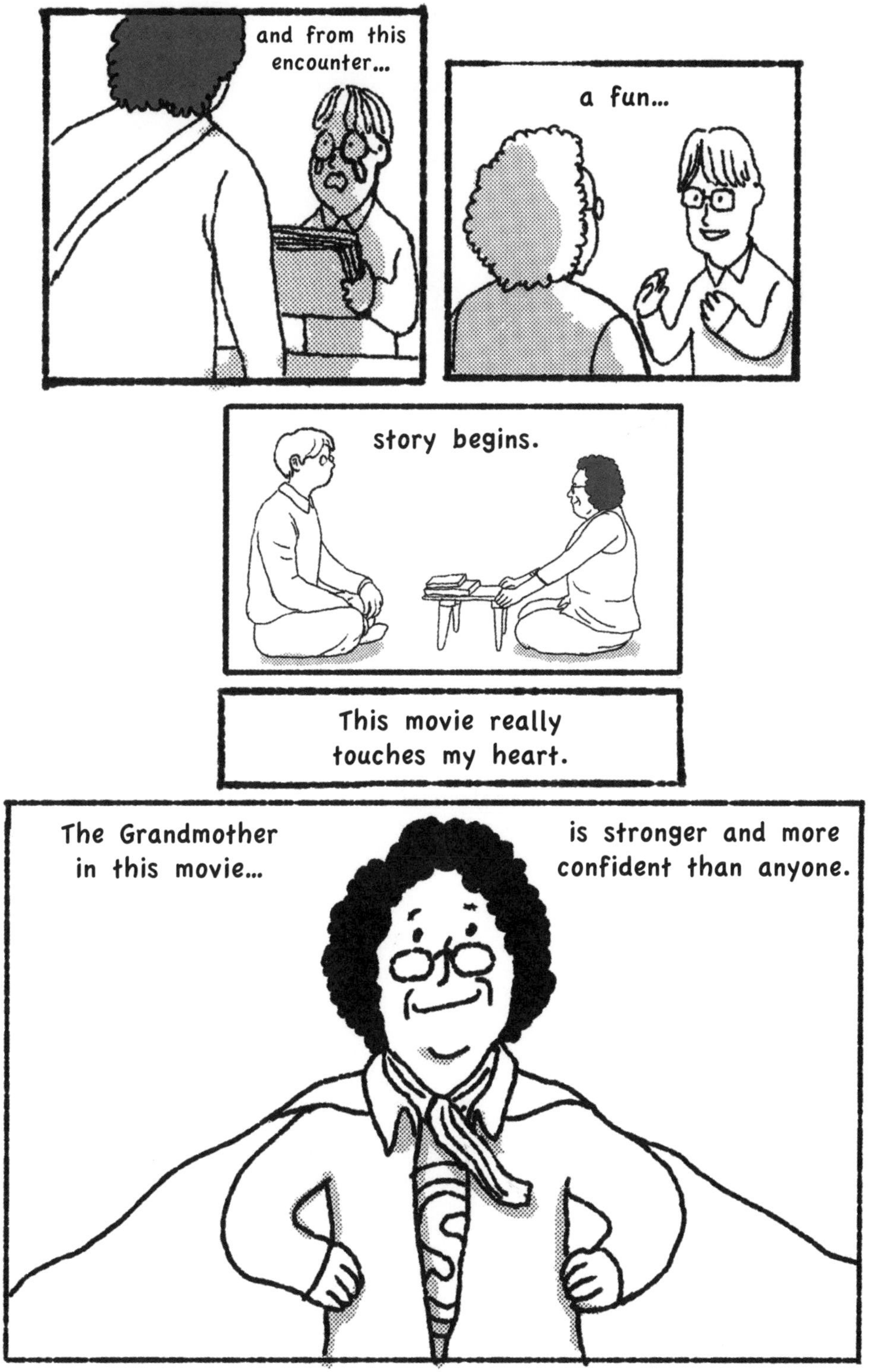
and from this encounter...
a fun...
story begins.
This movie really touches my heart.
The Grandmother in this movie...
is stronger and more confident than anyone.

Our Grandmothers in life are similar to the movie's main character.

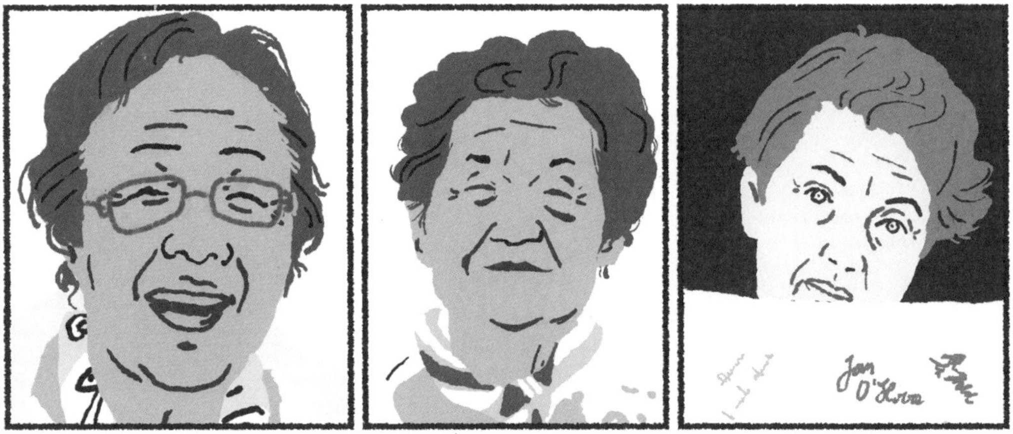
Jan O'Herne

Grandmother Lee Yong-soo | Grandmother Kim Gun-ja | Grandmother Jan Ruff O'Herne

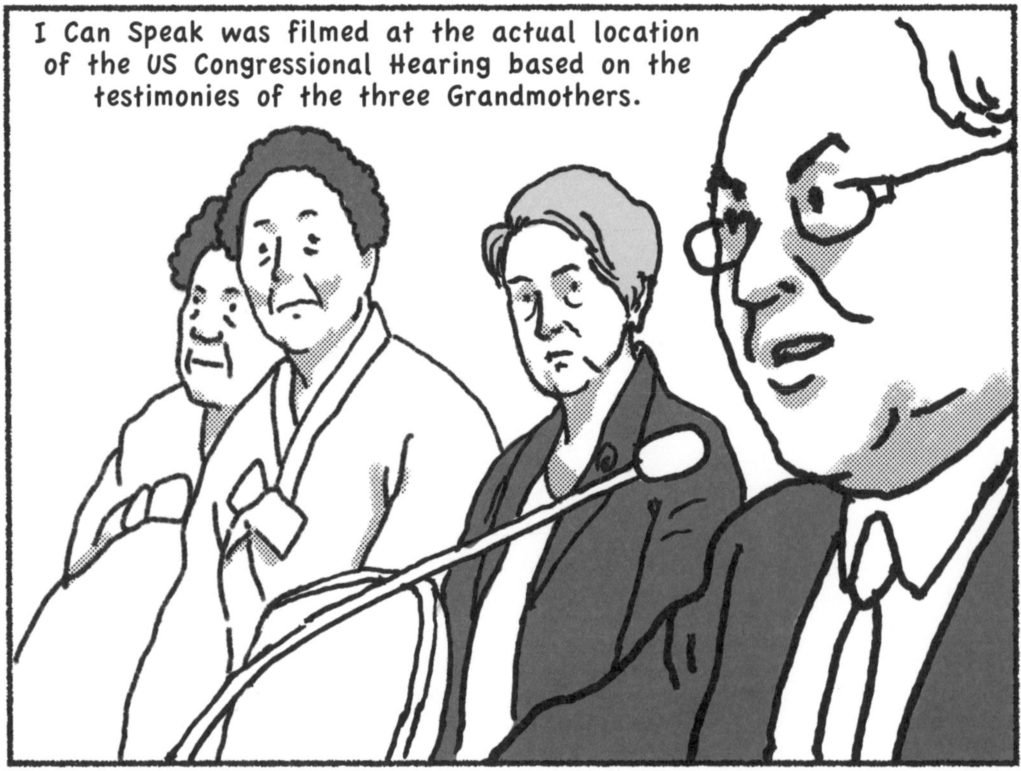
I Can Speak was filmed at the actual location of the US Congressional Hearing based on the testimonies of the three Grandmothers.

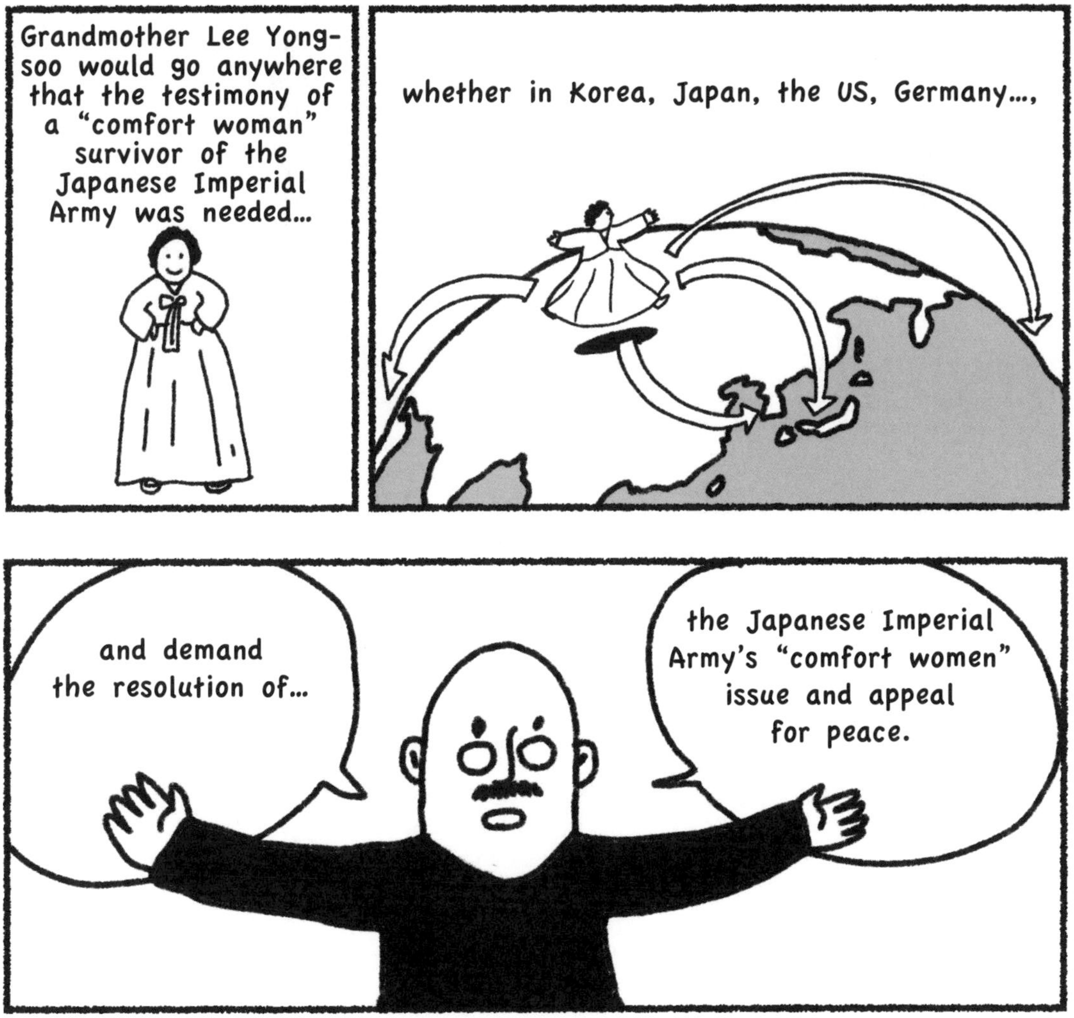
Grandmother Lee Yong-soo would go anywhere that the testimony of a "comfort woman" survivor of the Japanese Imperial Army was needed...
whether in Korea, Japan, the US, Germany...,
and demand the resolution of...
the Japanese Imperial Army's "comfort women" issue and appeal for peace.

A Story of a Japanese Human Rights Activist

Grandmother Lee Yong-soo and Misseuko Nobukawa

Misseuko Nobukawa, a housewife, has been helping "comfort women" survivors in both Japan and Korea while traveling back and forth.

She has known the Grandmothers since 1994.

Ms. Nobukawa had had no interest in the war Japan had started. Although she was shocked when she heard war stories at the age of 20 at a local clinic, she just accepted it.

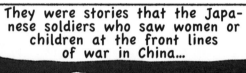

They were stories that the Japanese soldiers who saw women or children at the front lines of war in China...

cruelly assaulted and killed them...

That war...

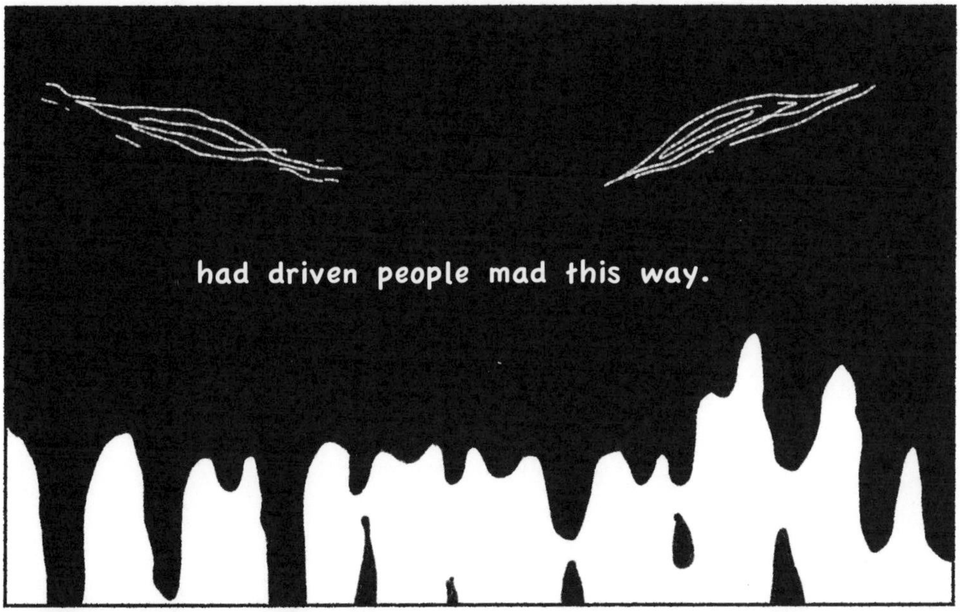
had driven people mad this way.

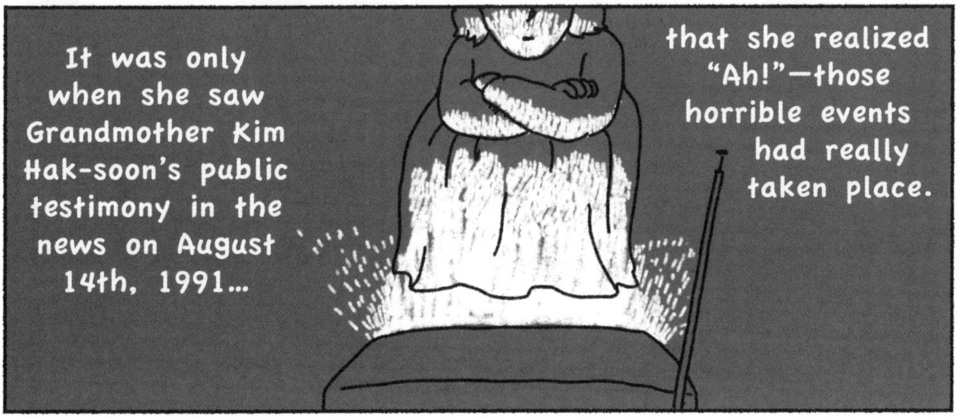
It was only when she saw Grandmother Kim Hak-soon's public testimony in the news on August 14th, 1991...
that she realized "Ah!"—those horrible events had really taken place.

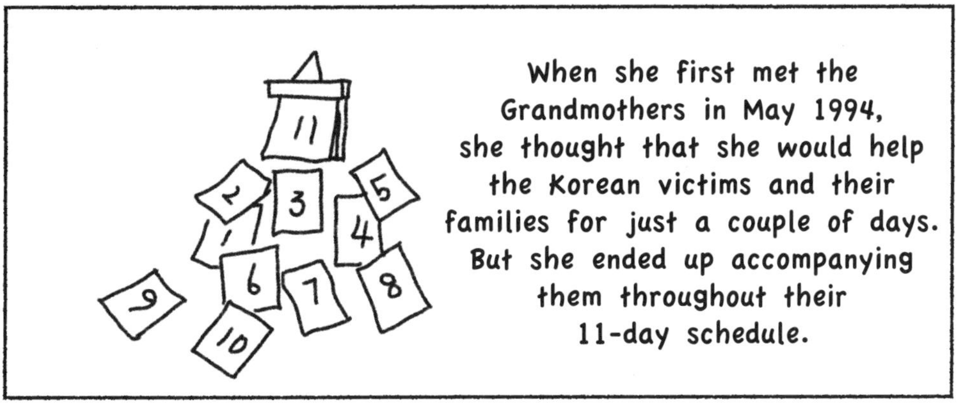
11
2
3
5
1
4
6
7
8
9
10
When she first met the Grandmothers in May 1994, she thought that she would help the Korean victims and their families for just a couple of days. But she ended up accompanying them throughout their 11-day schedule.

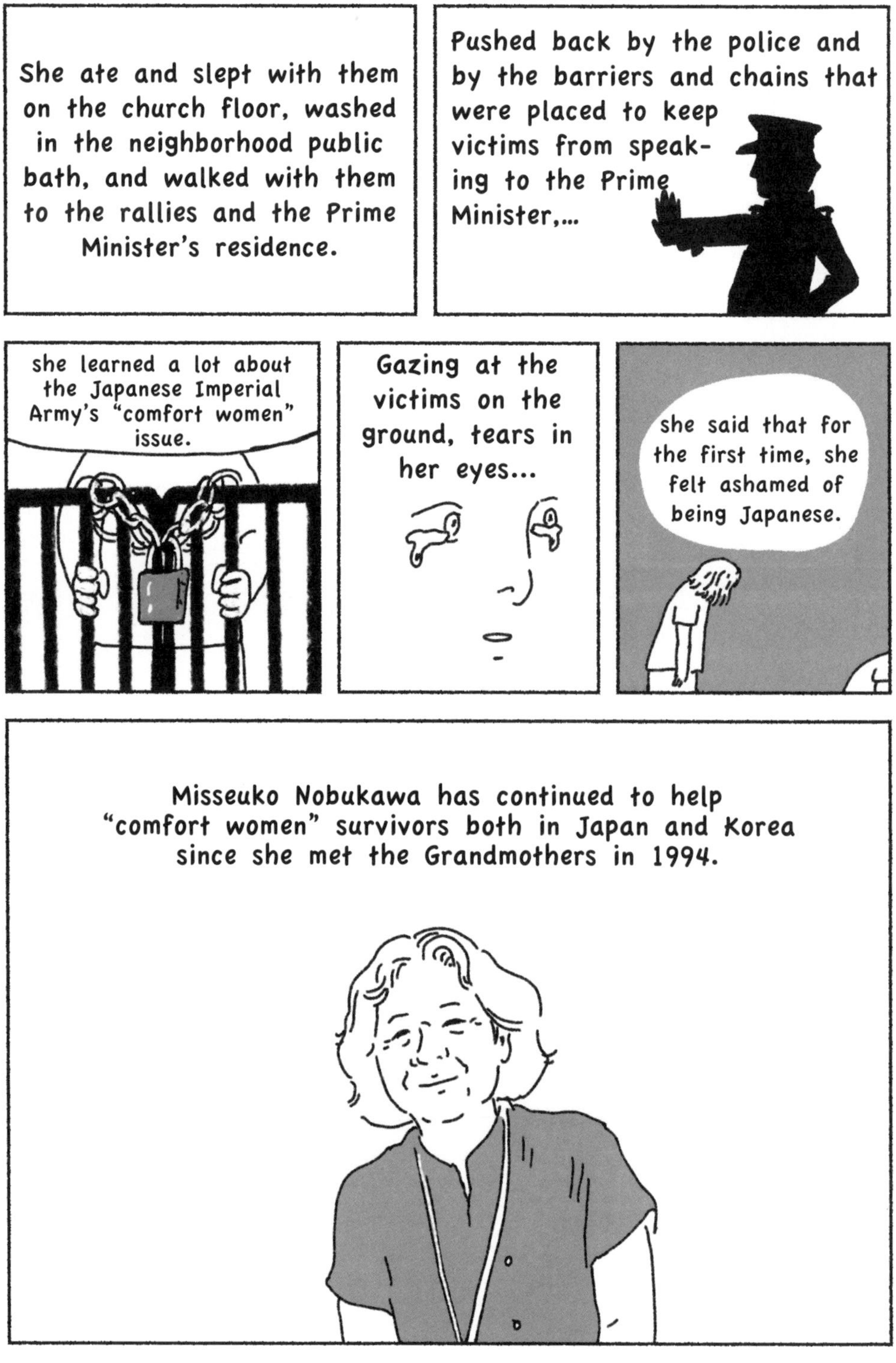
She ate and slept with them on the church floor, washed in the neighborhood public bath, and walked with them to the rallies and the Prime Minister's residence.
Pushed back by the police and by the barriers and chains that were placed to keep victims from speak-ing to the Prime Minister,...
she learned a lot about the Japanese Imperial Army's "comfort women" issue.
Gazing at the victims on the ground, tears in her eyes...
she said that for the first time, she felt ashamed of being Japanese.
Misseuko Nobukawa has continued to help "comfort women" survivors both in Japan and Korea since she met the Grandmothers in 1994.

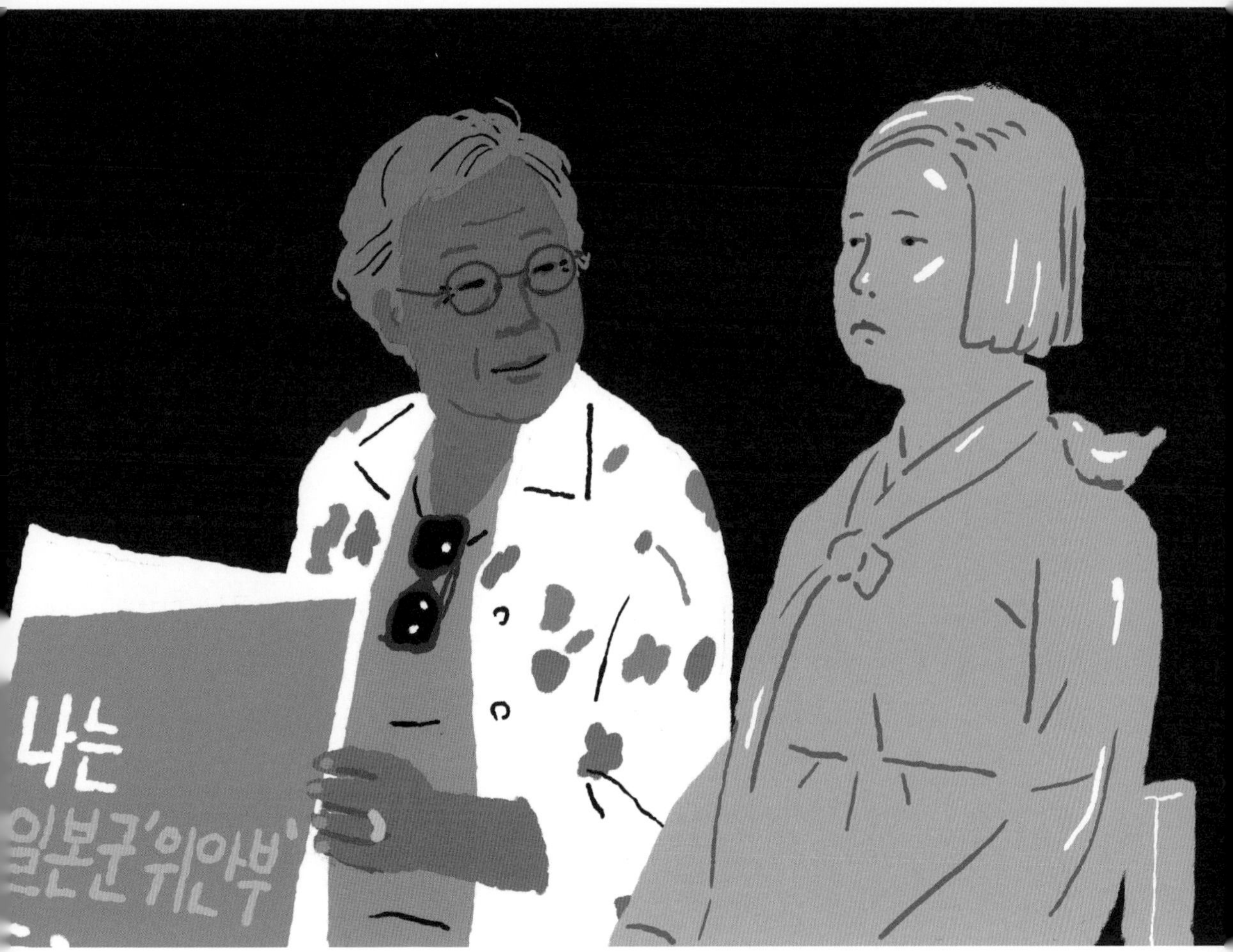
나는
일본군'위안부'

Most particularly, she has accompanied Grandmother Lee Yong-soo to her testimonial events. The two have been together for more than 100 events.

*This sign reads "One of the 'Japanese Military Comfort Women'"

Sometimes, they get upset with each other.

But the next day, they get along.

Memorial Day, a Time to Be Together

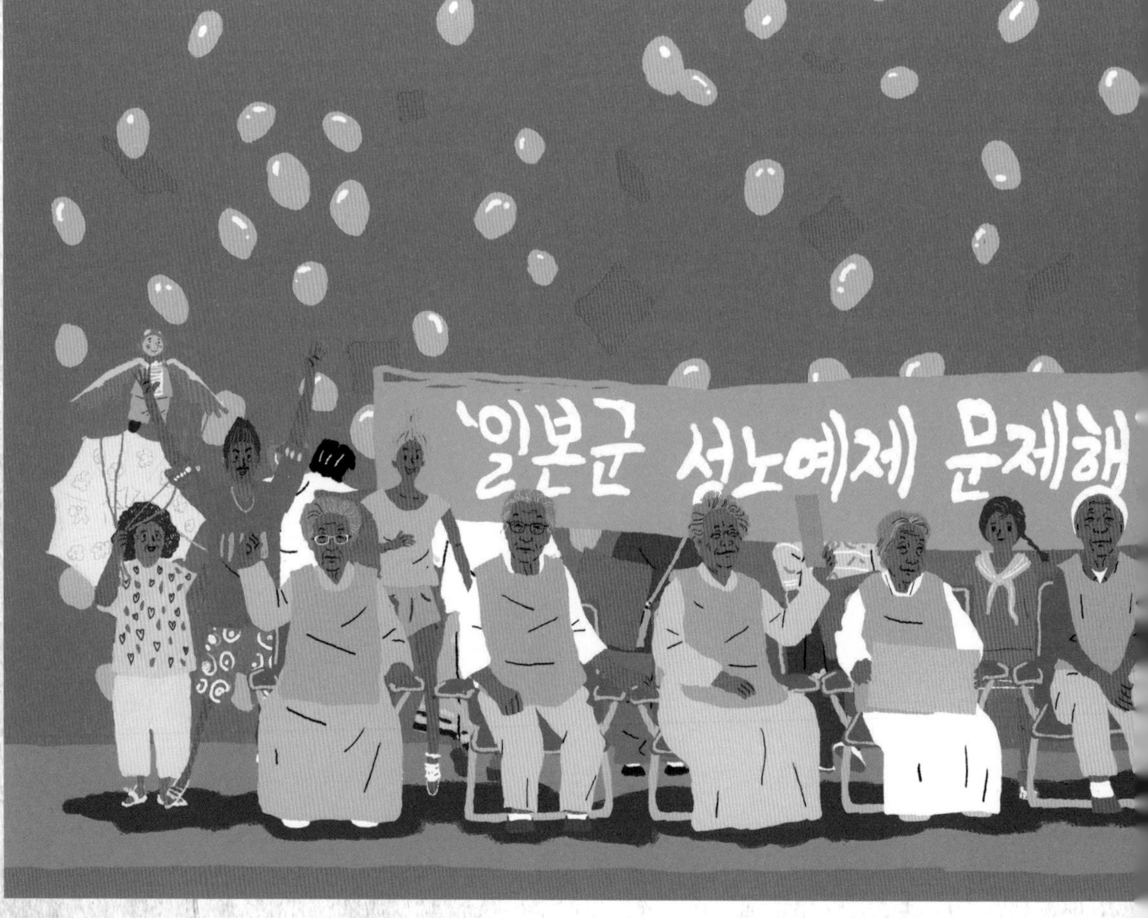

'일본군 성노예제 문제해

August 14th, 2019, the "7th World Memorial Day for 'Comfort Women' of the Japanese Imperial Army".

Our 1400th Demand for a Resolution to the Japapnese Imperial Army "Comfort Women" Problem

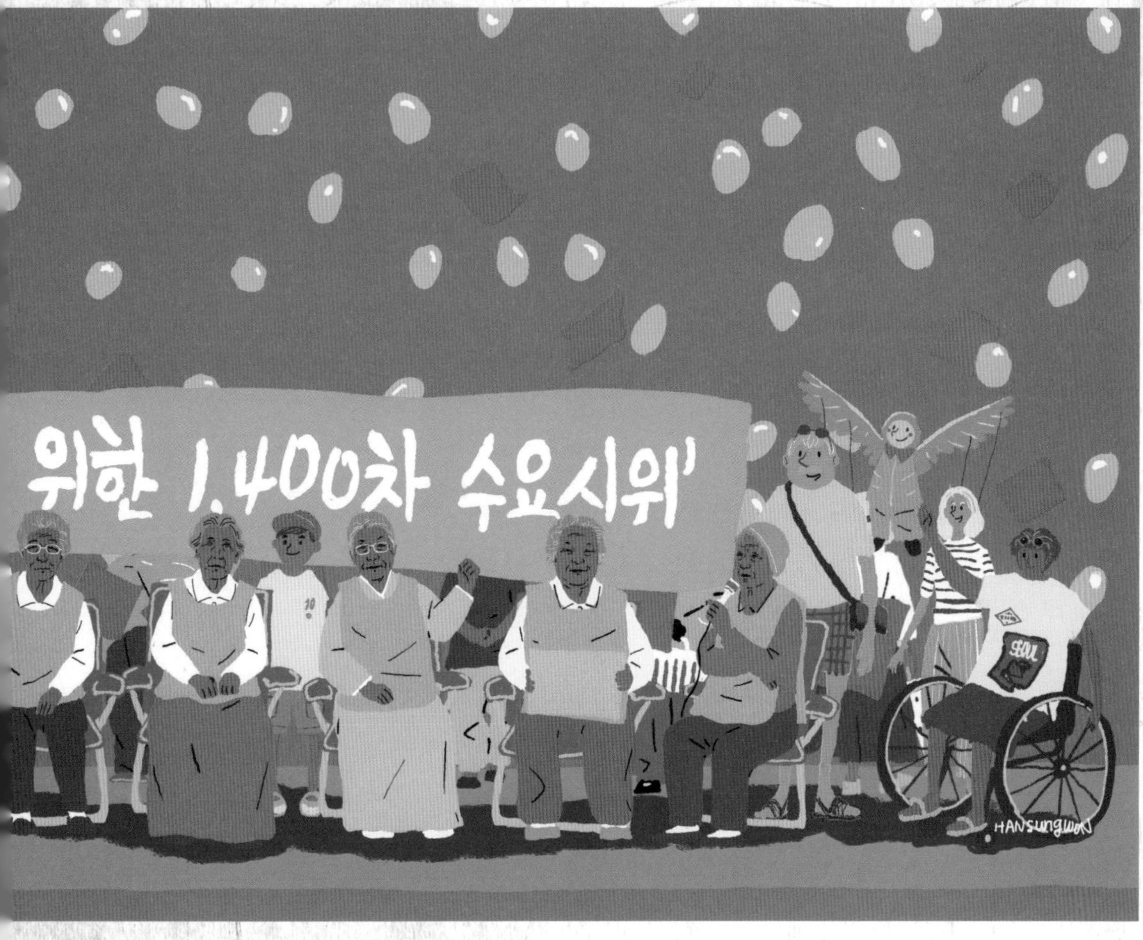
위한 1,400차 수요시위'
HANSungwon

The Wednesday Protests which began in 1992
is the longest running single protest in the world.

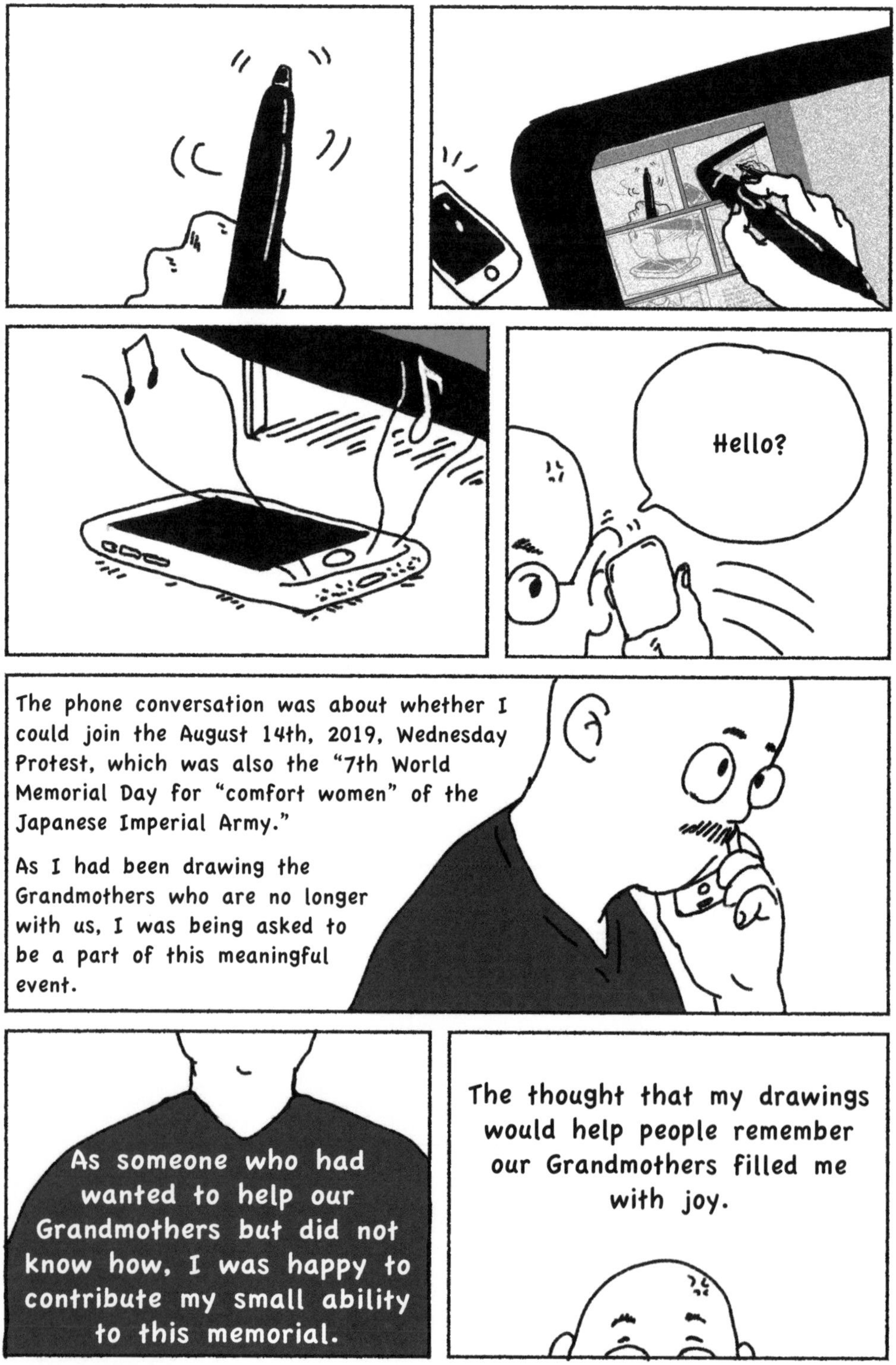

Hello?
The phone conversation was about whether I could join the August 14th, 2019, Wednesday Protest, which was also the "7th World Memorial Day for "comfort women" of the Japanese Imperial Army."
As I had been drawing the Grandmothers who are no longer with us, I was being asked to be a part of this meaningful event.
As someone who had wanted to help our Grandmothers but did not know how, I was happy to contribute my small ability to this memorial.
The thought that my drawings would help people remember our Grandmothers filled me with joy.

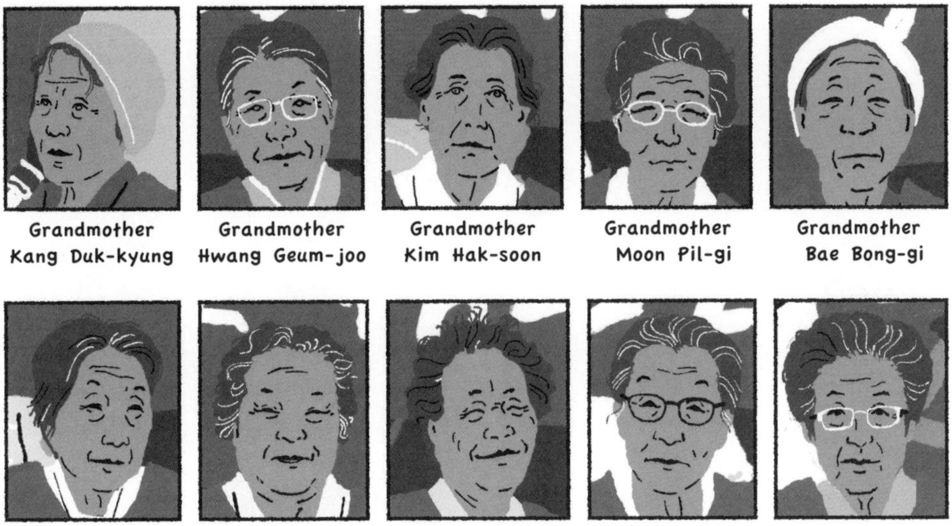

Grandmother Kang Duk-kyung
Grandmother Hwang Geum-joo
Grandmother Kim Hak-soon
Grandmother Moon Pil-gi
Grandmother Bae Bong-gi
Grandmother Pak Young-shim
Grandmother Ahn Jeom-soon
Grandmother Song Shin-do
Grandmother Kim Bok-dong
Grandmother Jung Suh-eun

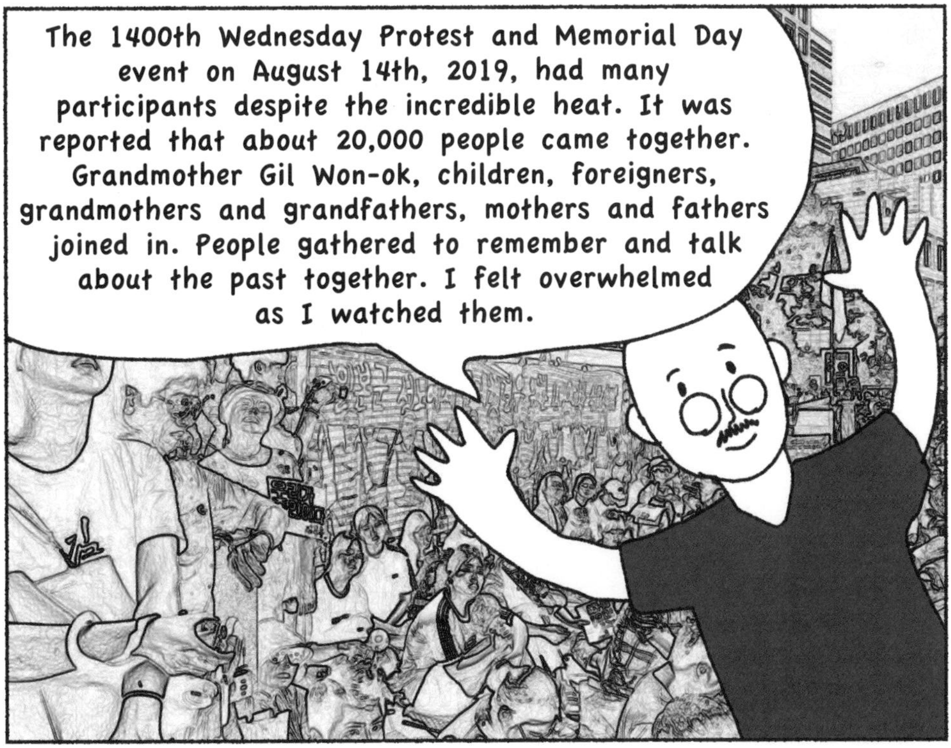
The 1400th Wednesday Protest and Memorial Day event on August 14th, 2019, had many participants despite the incredible heat. It was reported that about 20,000 people came together. Grandmother Gil Won-ok, children, foreigners, grandmothers and grandfathers, mothers and fathers joined in. People gathered to remember and talk about the past together. I felt overwhelmed as I watched them.

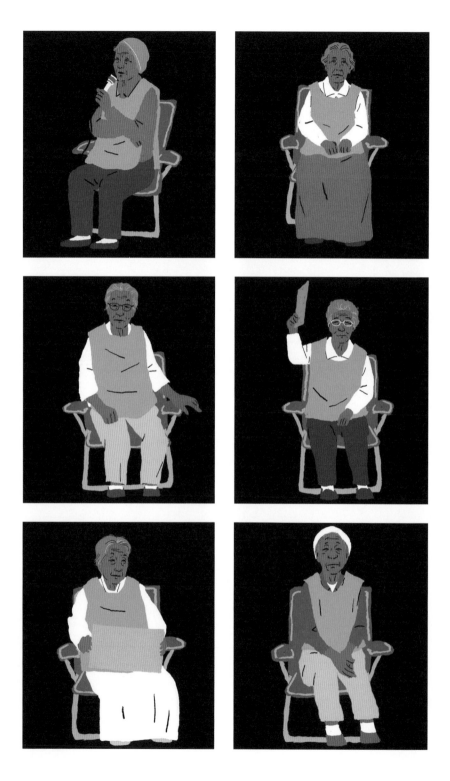

We call out our Grandmothers' names.

Grandmother Kang Duk-kyung,
Grandmother Kim Hak-soon, Grandmother Kim Bok-dong,
Grandmother Moon Pil-gi, Grandmother Pak Young-shim,
Grandmother Bae Bong-gi, Grandmother Song Shin-do, Grandmother Jung
Suh-eun, Grandmother Ahn Jeom-soon, Grandmother Hwang Geum-joo.

We always carry you in our hearts. You are as with
us now as you were when you sat among us.

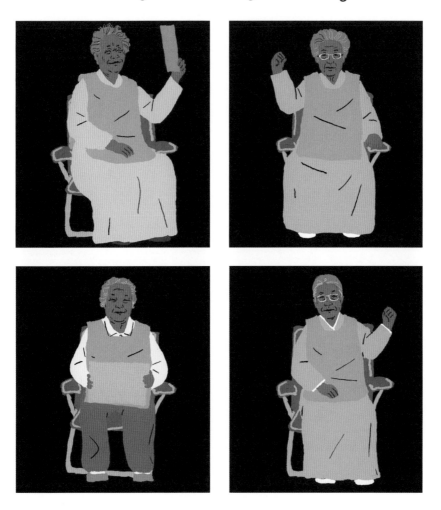

"I am 93 years old, victim Kim Bok-dong.
They said I had to make military uniforms. I had to work in a factory
that lacked workers. If I refused, then they would take everything
and my family would be chased away. But the truth was,
I was taken to the 'comfort station' for soldiers."

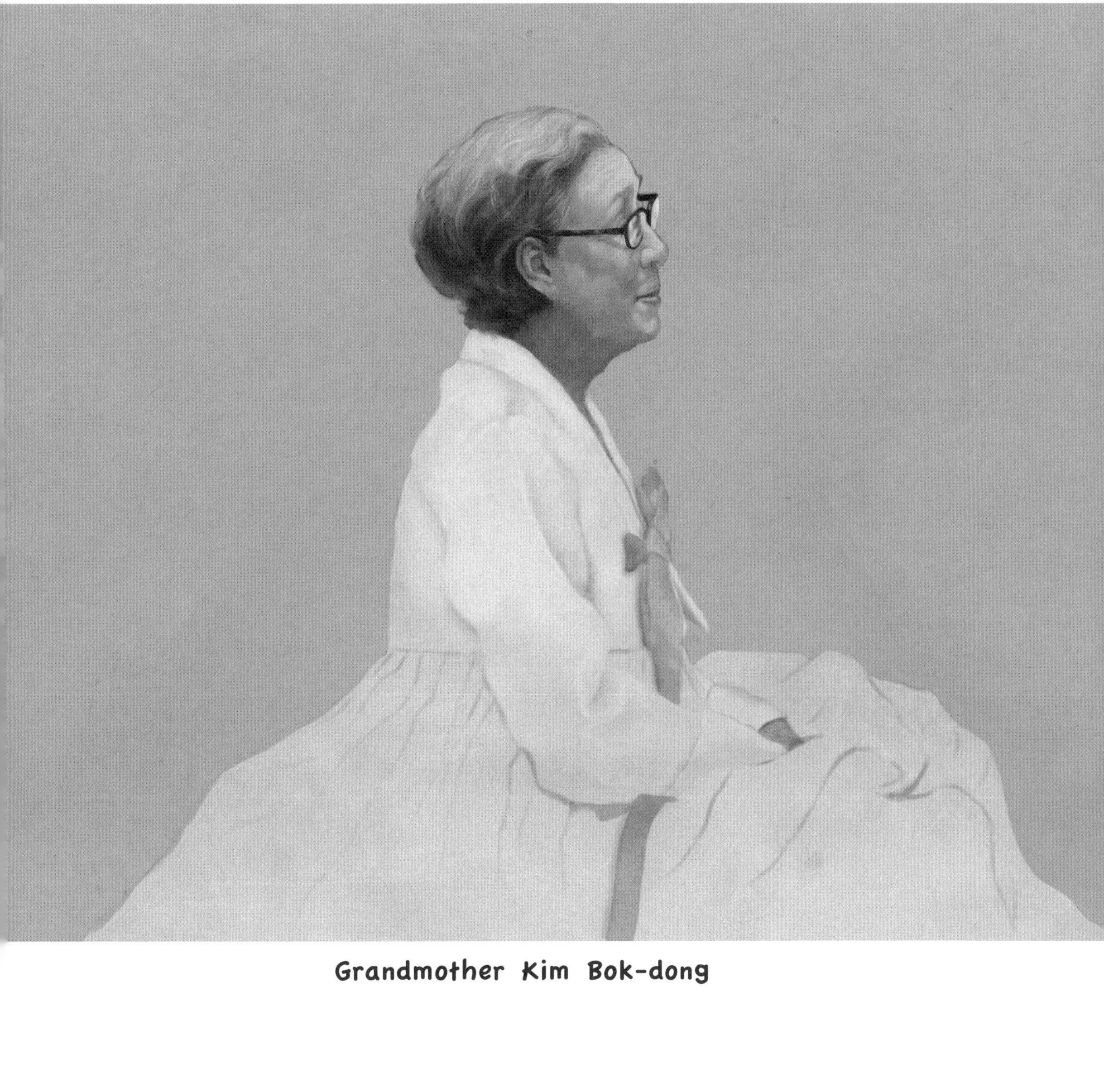

Grandmother Kim Bok-dong

"Songs are better because where there are
songs there's a reason to smile. This is better than gossiping
and complaining about others."

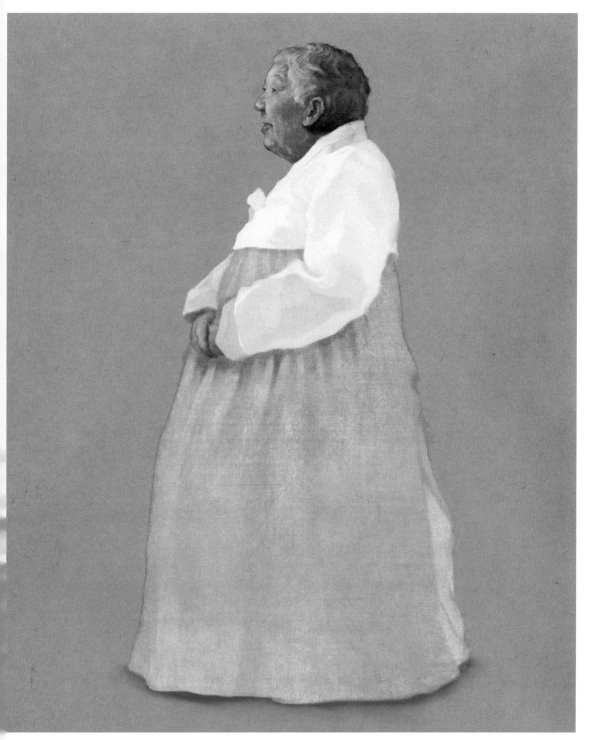

Grandmother Gil Won-ok

"Your money cannot restore the youth you stole from me."
The Japanese government is still unrepentant of their past crimes
and Grandmother Ahn Jeom-soon worked as a human rights activist
from 2002 and asked the Japanese government for a clear
and direct apology.

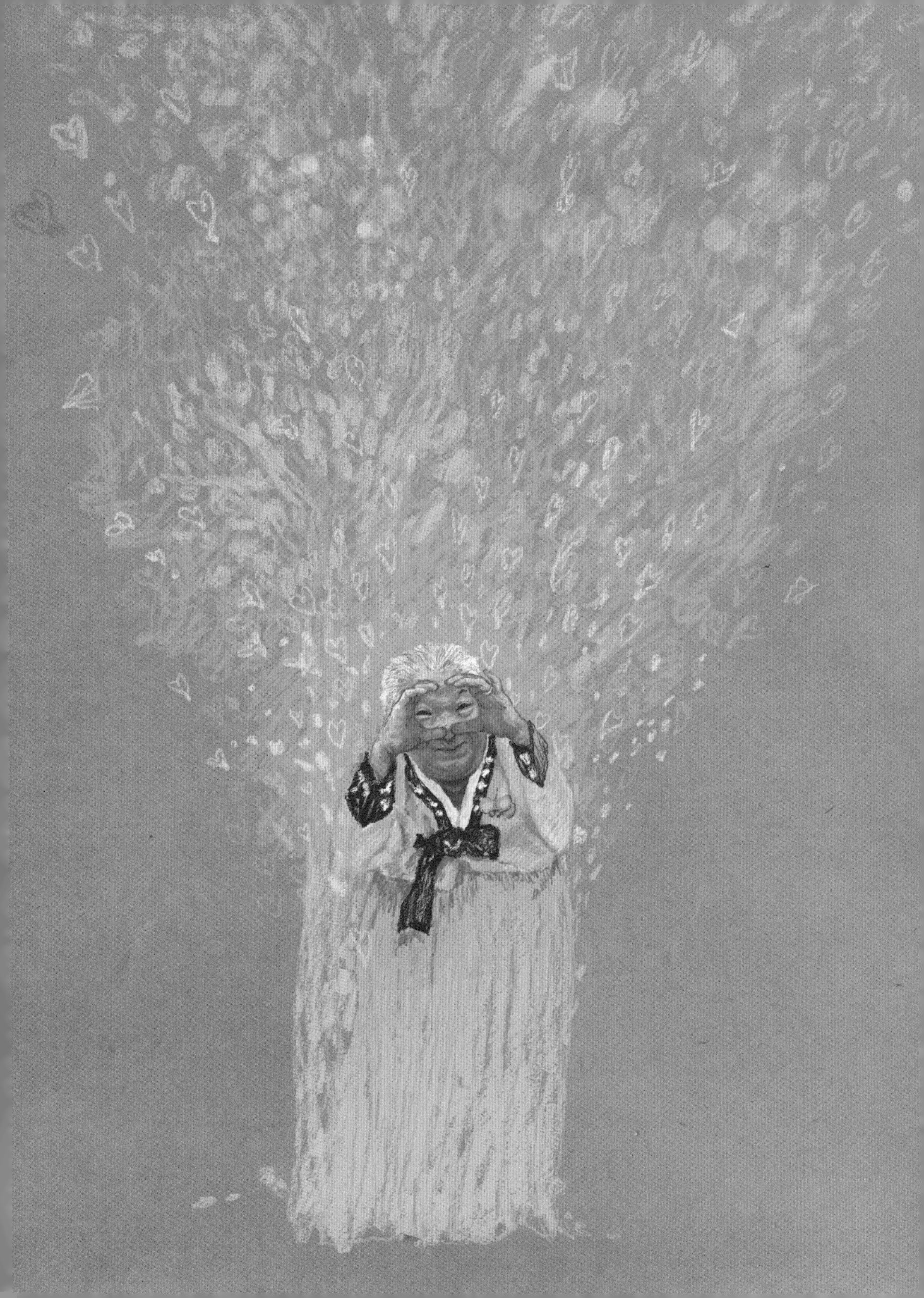

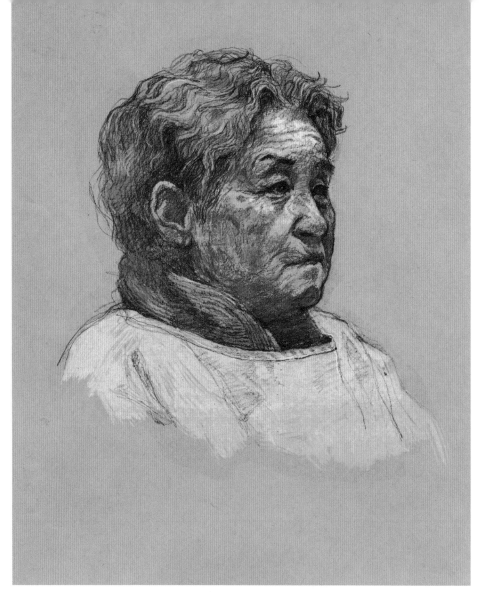

Grandmother Park Ok-ryun

She was forced to work as a "comfort woman" for three years in Papua New Guinea in the South Pacific. In 2007, she testified via a digital video so that the US House of Representatives passed a resolution asking the Japanese government make a formal apology to former "comfort women."

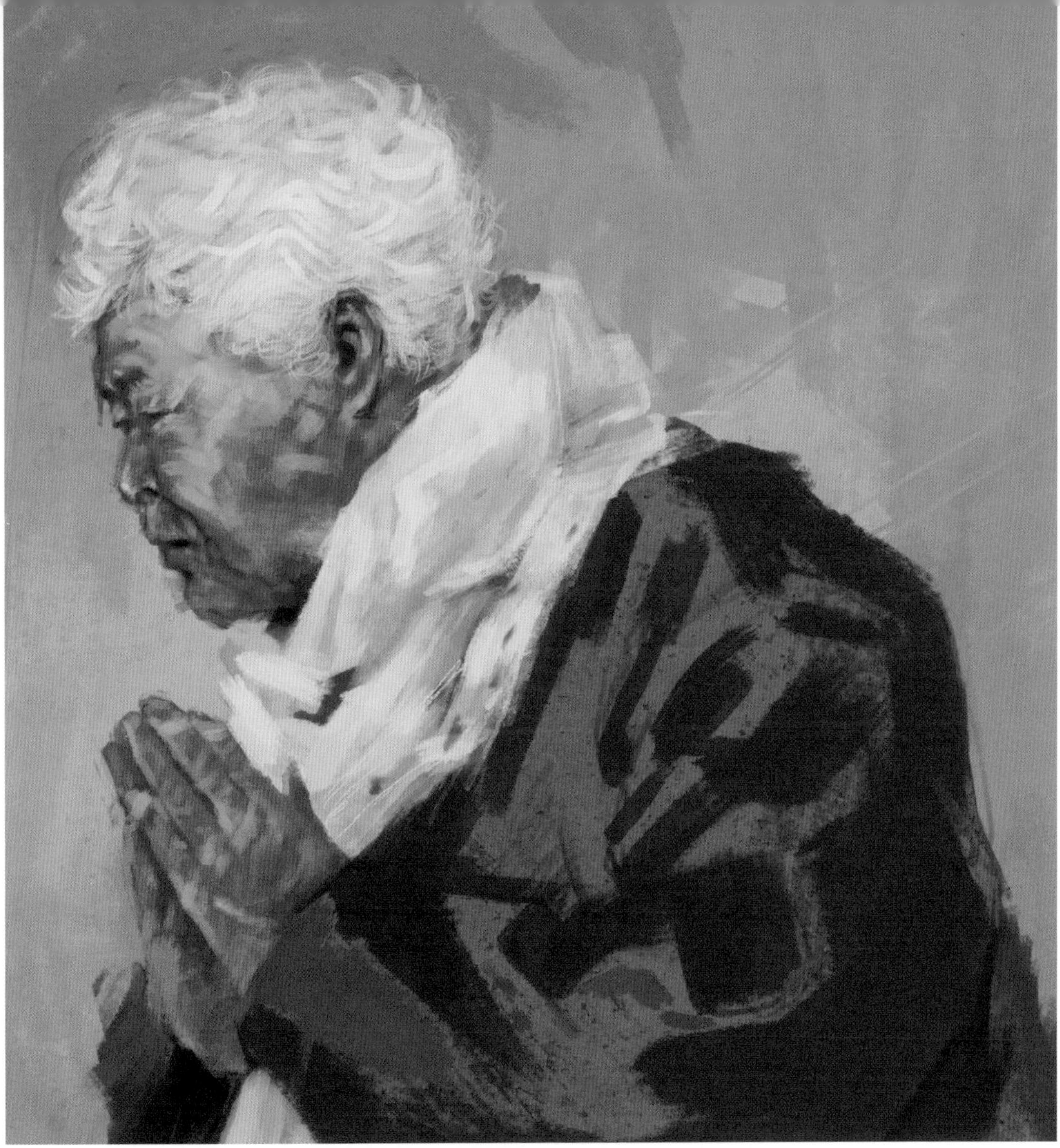

Grandmother Lee Ok-seon

"The Japanese government needs to apologize to the Grandmothers who are still alive. If they refuse, then I ask them to give back to me the 15-year-old Lee Ok-seon." Grandmother Lee became a "comfort woman" at 15 and was retained in a station in China. By the time she return to Korea, 60 years after liberation, she was considered a dead person because her mother had filed her death certificate believing her child had passed away.

Grandmother Park Dae-im was forcefully taken as a "comfort woman" for the Japanese Imperial Army when she was 22 in 1934. Throughout the years, she had held onto the alien residence card issued by the Chinese government in 1957 as this was the only document that could verify her identity. She never forgot her homeland and wanted to return. While touching Korea on the map, she expressed her longing and her wish to return even if only after her death to be buried in her hometown.

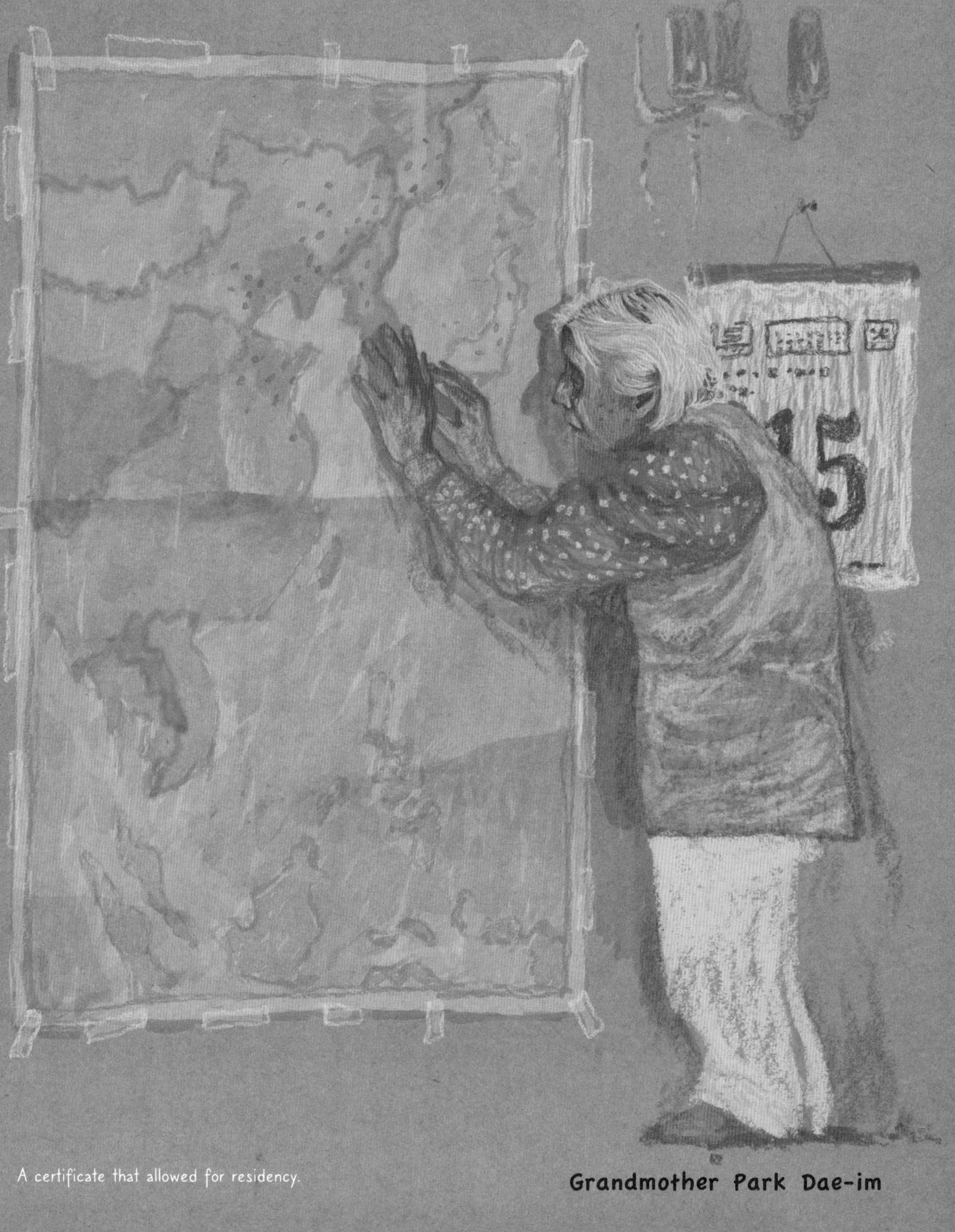
15

A certificate that allowed for residency.

Grandmother Park Dae-im

"I wish the Japanese government would apologize
while I am alive and promise never to make war."
Grandmother passed away at age 96 on May 17th, 2016.

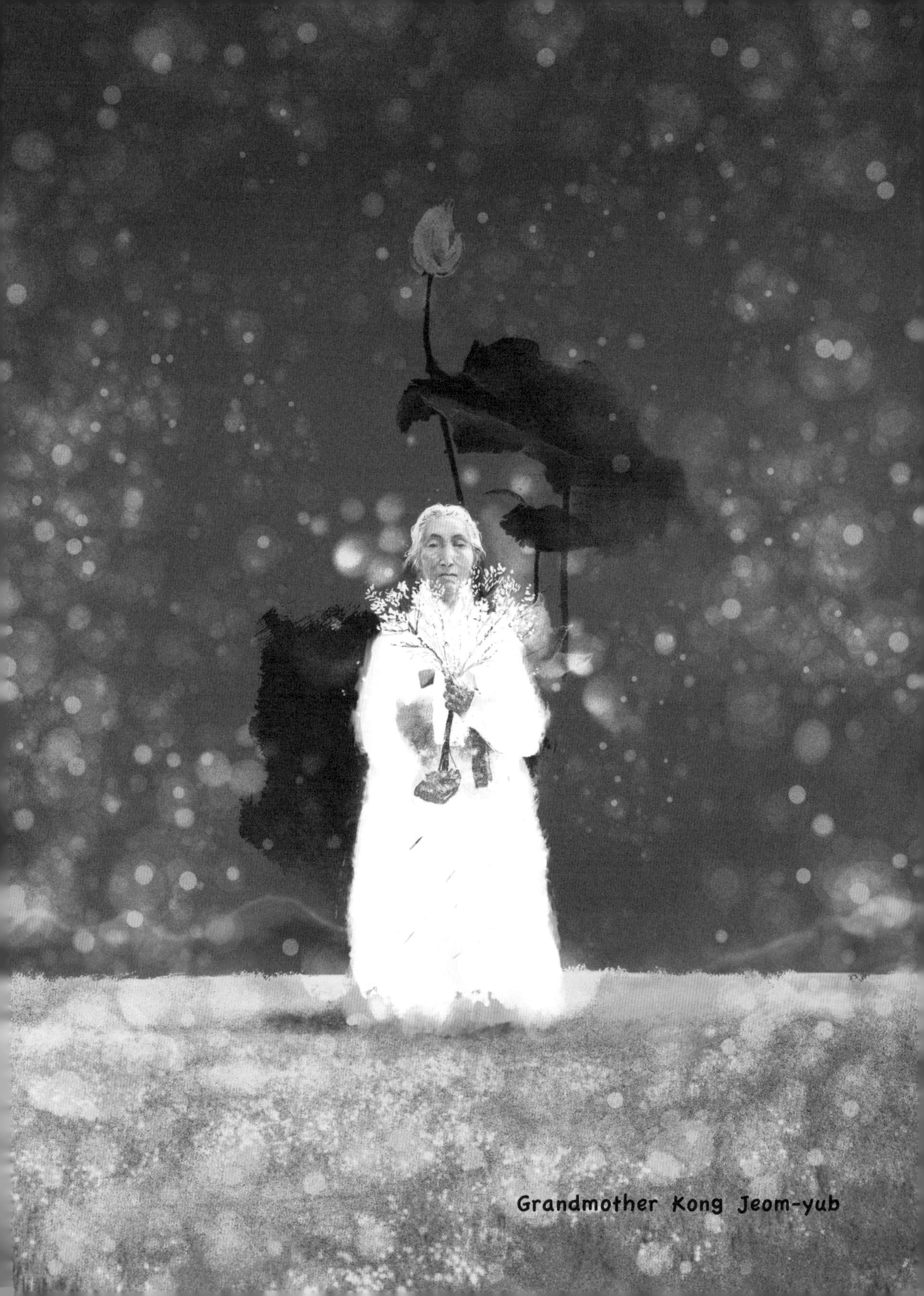
Grandmother Kong Jeom-yub

We Remember Our Grandmothers

There are those Grandmothers we do not know,

who are ashamed of the past
who do not wish to remember
who forgot their mother tongue,
and who for many other painful
reasons cannot step forward.

There are many we do not know.

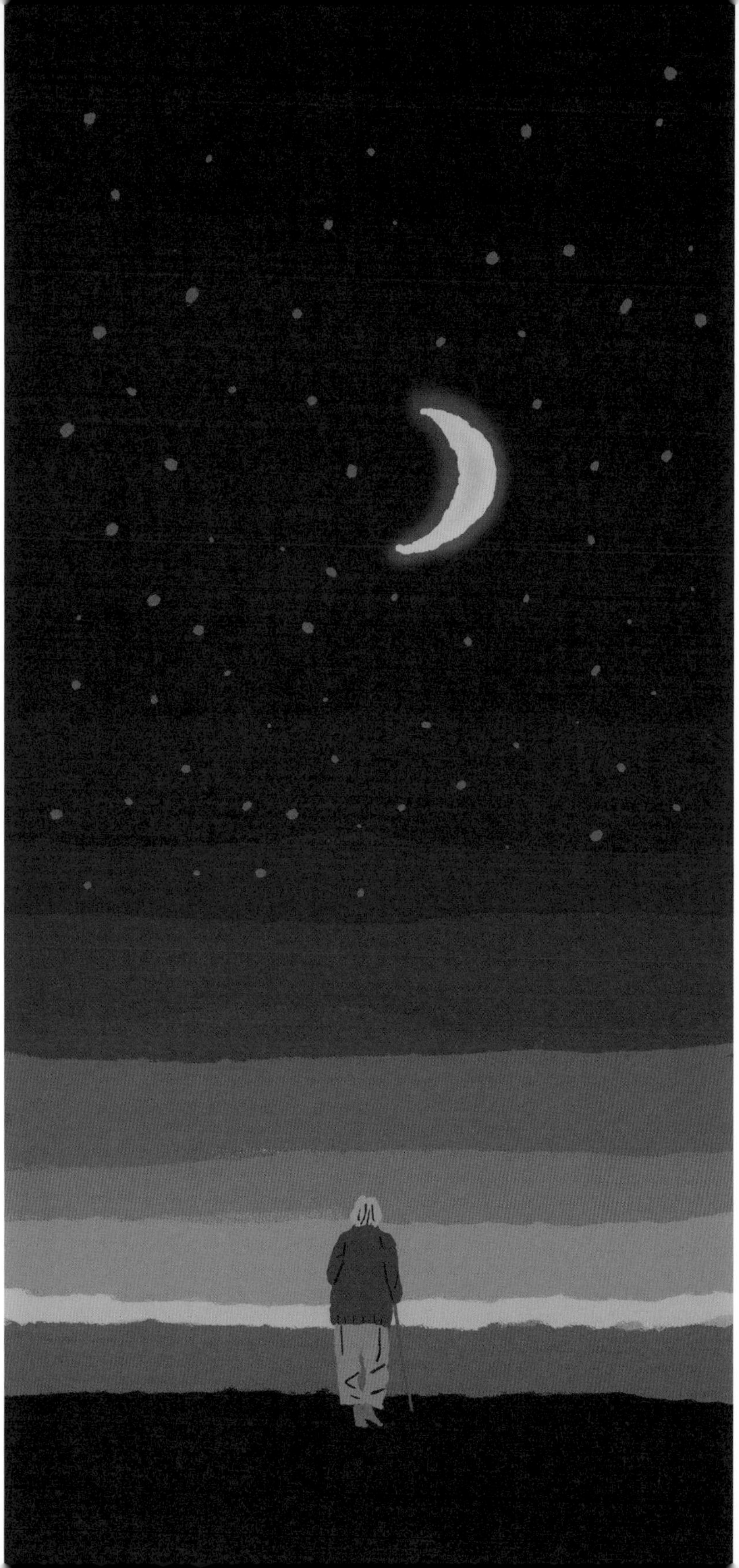

Because they don't want to remember

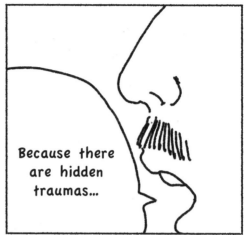

Because there are hidden traumas...

My heart breaks to think of so many Grandmothers who keep silent.

But this is understandable.

A book described Grandmother Kim Hak-soon's testimony as "the most beautiful and courageous confession in the world."

The book's title translates as *25 Years of Wednesdays*

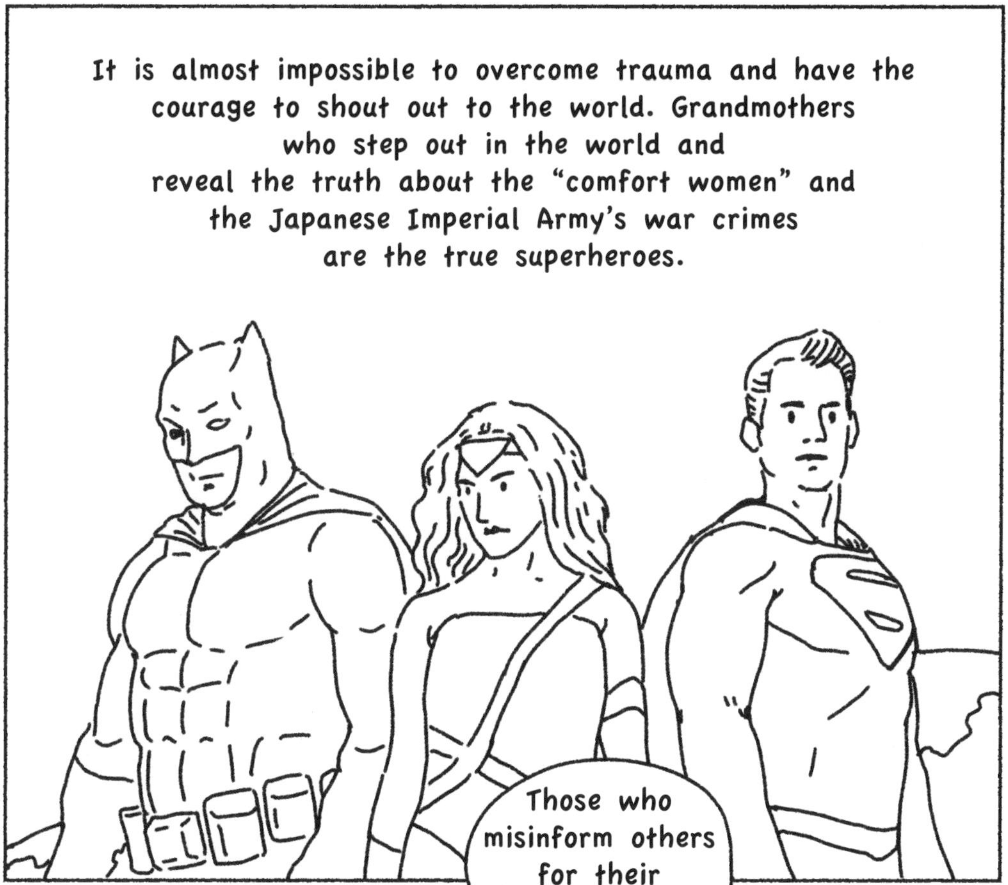
It is almost impossible to overcome trauma and have the courage to shout out to the world. Grandmothers who step out in the world and reveal the truth about the "comfort women" and the Japanese Imperial Army's war crimes are the true superheroes.

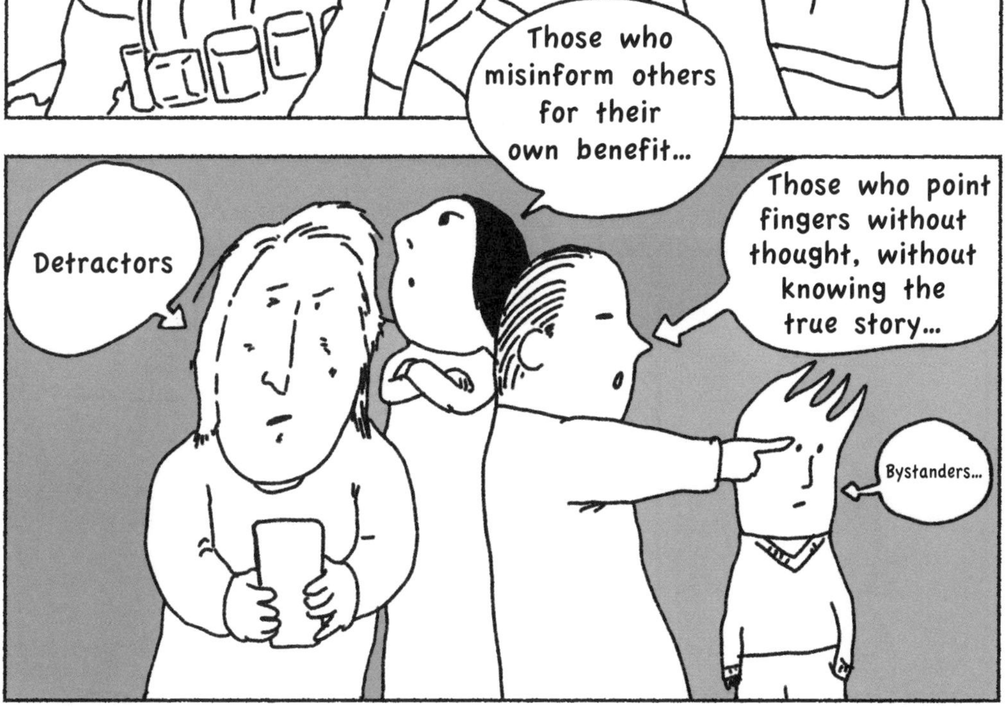
Detractors
Those who misinform others for their own benefit...
Those who point fingers without thought, without knowing the true story...
Bystanders...

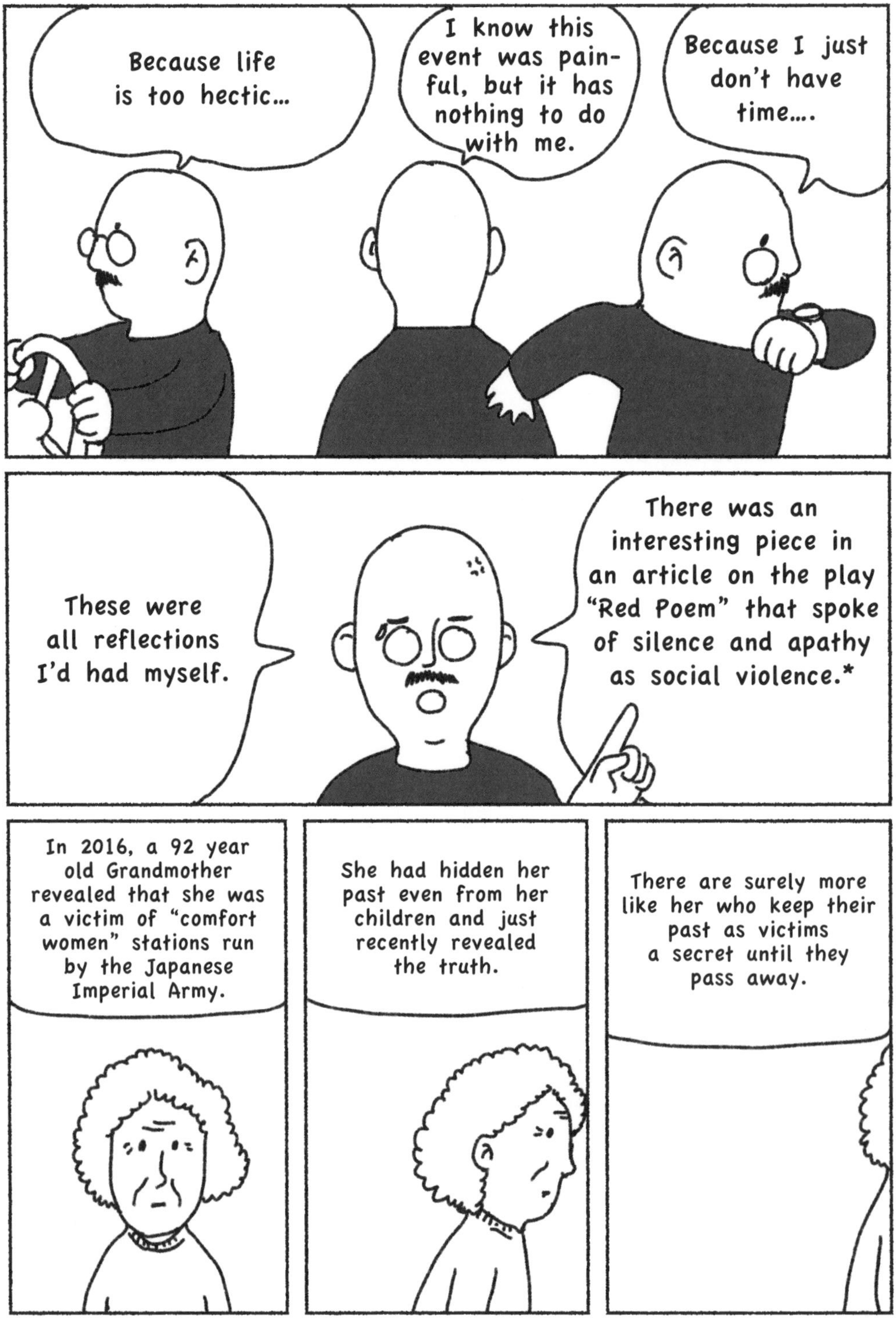
Because life is too hectic...
I know this event was painful, but it has nothing to do with me.
Because I just don't have time....
These were all reflections I'd had myself.
There was an interesting piece in an article on the play "Red Poem" that spoke of silence and apathy as social violence.*
In 2016, a 92 year old Grandmother revealed that she was a victim of "comfort women" stations run by the Japanese Imperial Army.
She had hidden her past even from her children and just recently revealed the truth.
There are surely more like her who keep their past as victims a secret until they pass away.

This statement comes from *25 Years of Wednesdays*.

I think of Grandmothers who cannot yet reveal their past
and commemorate them as I draw "Our Grandmothers
and Those Grandmothers We Do Not Know."

Leaving records through drawings and
words is what I do best.

Instead of hating those who caused this, I want to never
forget "Our Grandmothers" who were hurt by war.

Instead of one...

two...

Not only two, but many should gather to remember.

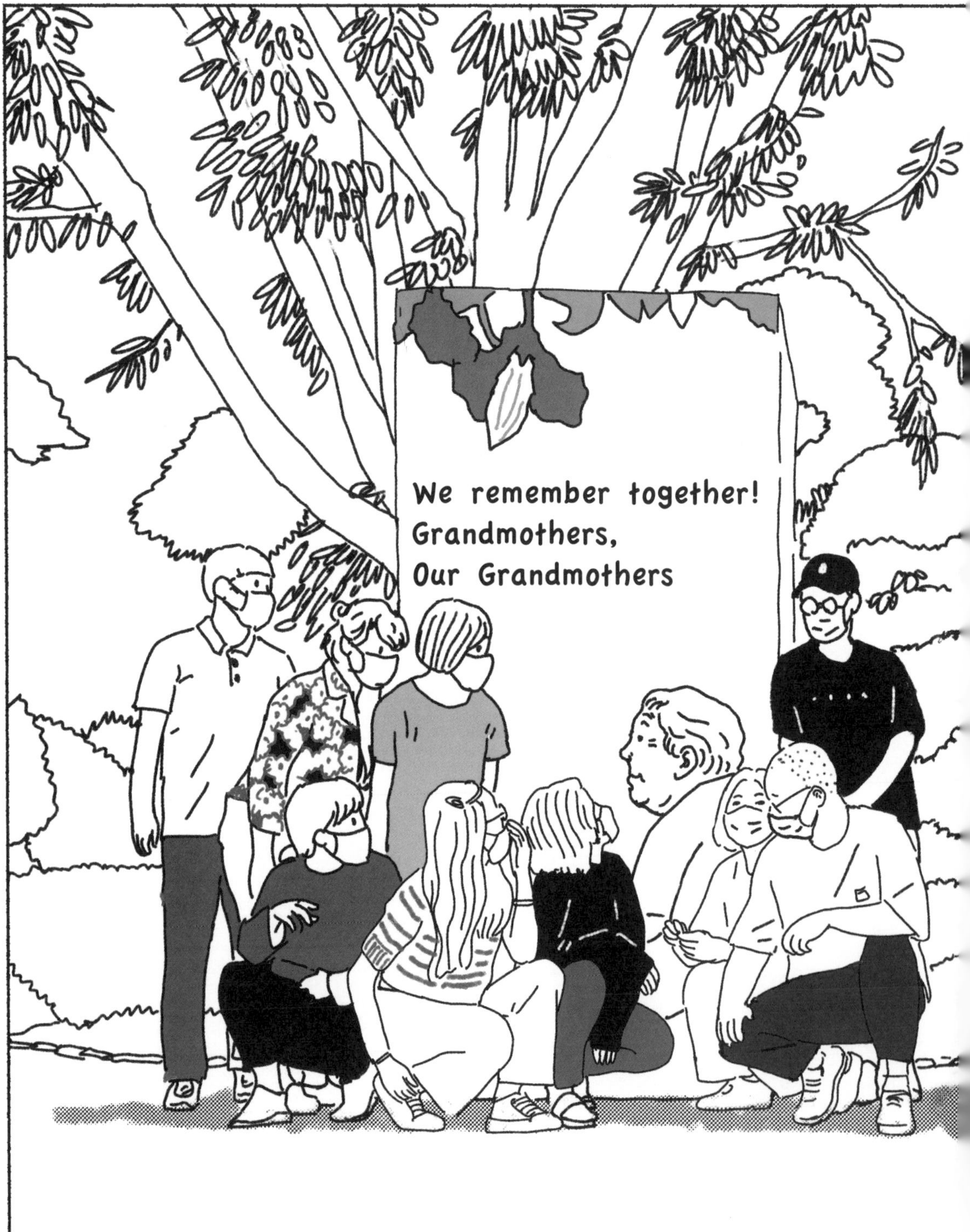
We remember together!
Grandmothers,
Our Grandmothers

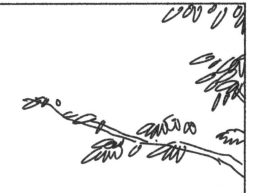

We love you, our Grandmothers.

* In this difficult time of the pandemic, we are still with you, our Grandmothers.

Epilogue

Through small actions, we honor and remember.

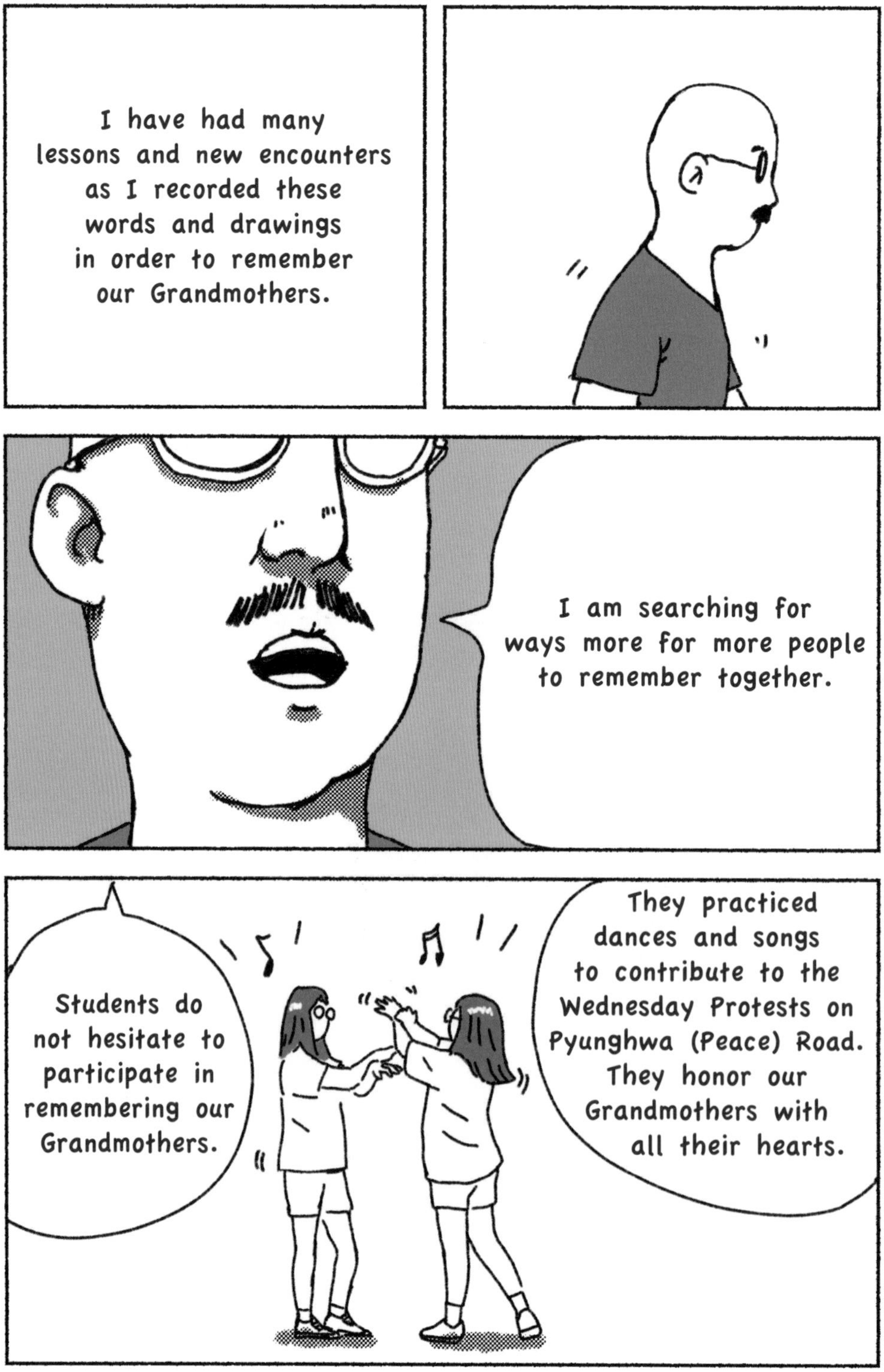
I have had many lessons and new encounters as I recorded these words and drawings in order to remember our Grandmothers.
I am searching for ways more for more people to remember together.
Students do not hesitate to participate in remembering our Grandmothers.
They practiced dances and songs to contribute to the Wednesday Protests on Pyunghwa (Peace) Road. They honor our Grandmothers with all their hearts.

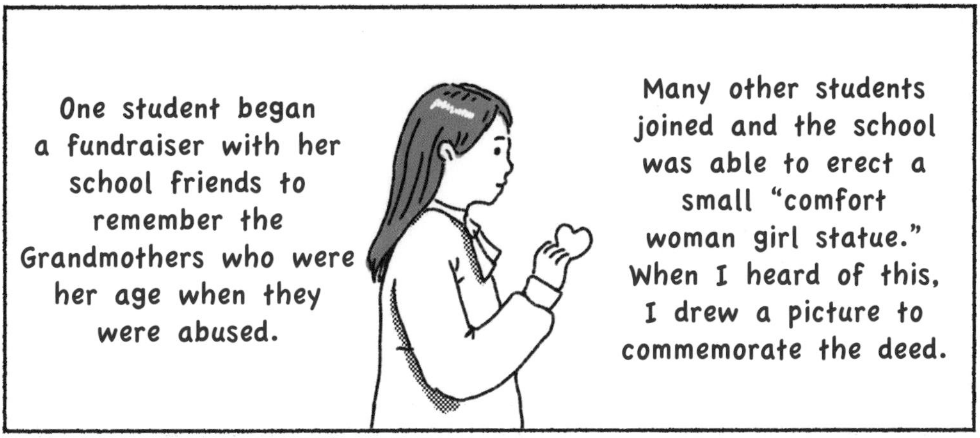
One student began a fundraiser with her school friends to remember the Grandmothers who were her age when they were abused.
Many other students joined and the school was able to erect a small "comfort woman girl statue." When I heard of this, I drew a picture to commemorate the deed.

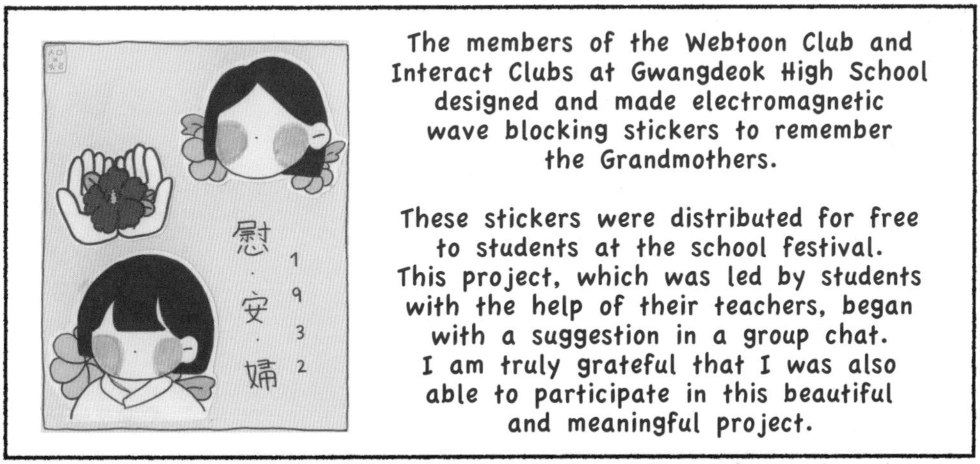
慰·安·婦
1932
The members of the Webtoon Club and Interact Clubs at Gwangdeok High School designed and made electromagnetic wave blocking stickers to remember the Grandmothers.
These stickers were distributed for free to students at the school festival. This project, which was led by students with the help of their teachers, began with a suggestion in a group chat. I am truly grateful that I was also able to participate in this beautiful and meaningful project.

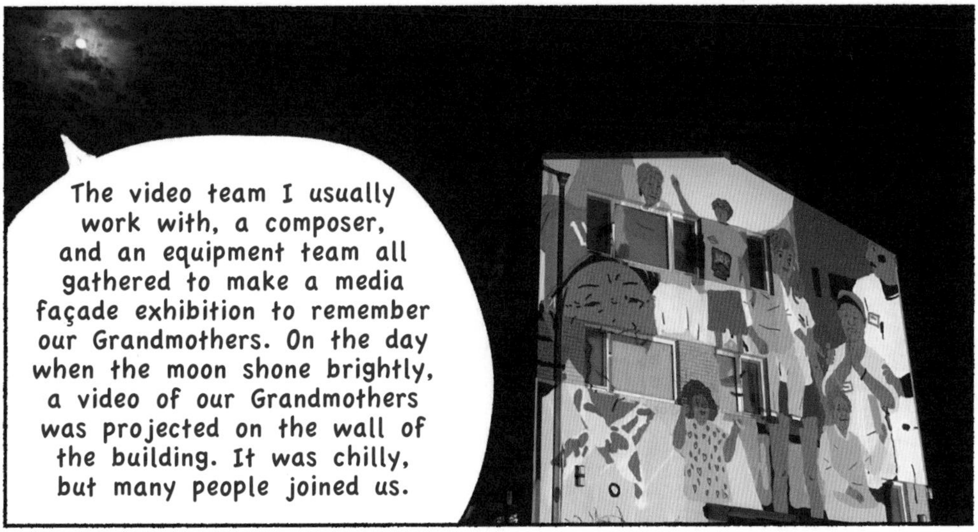
The video team I usually work with, a composer, and an equipment team all gathered to make a media façade exhibition to remember our Grandmothers. On the day when the moon shone brightly, a video of our Grandmothers was projected on the wall of the building. It was chilly, but many people joined us.

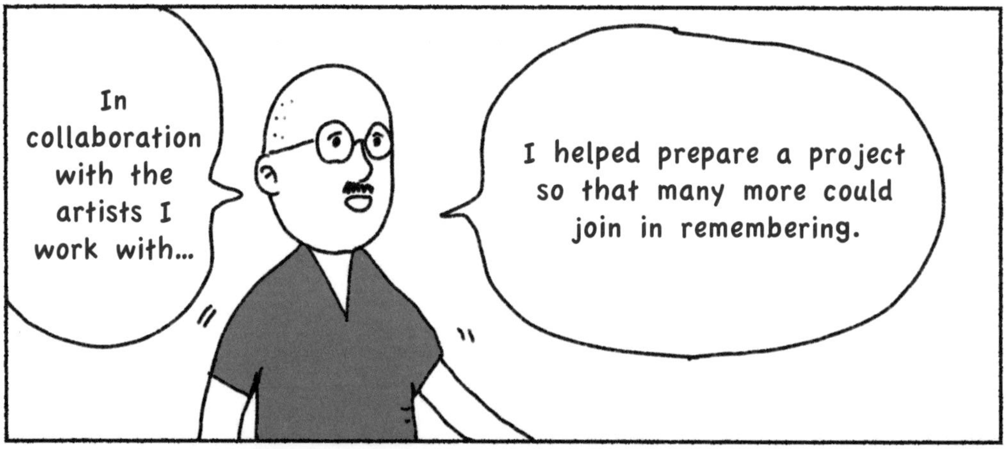
In collaboration with the artists I work with...
I helped prepare a project so that many more could join in remembering.

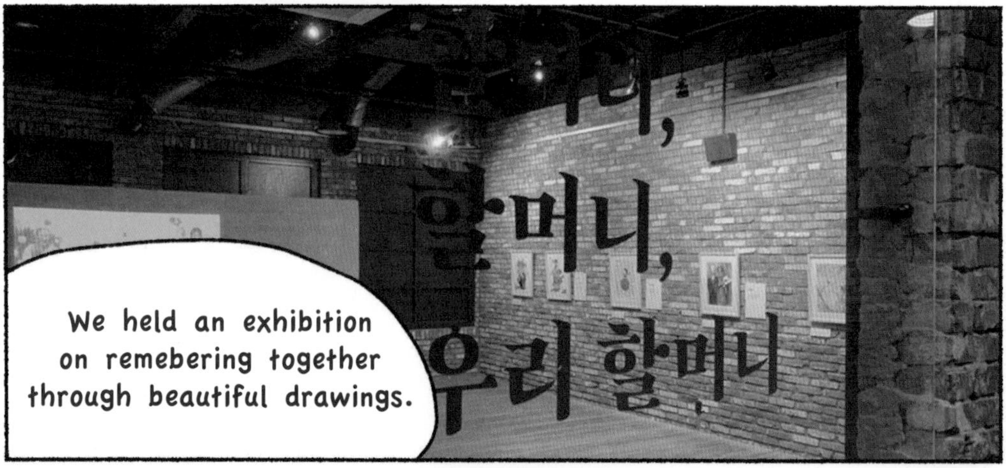
할머니,
우리 할머니
We held an exhibition on remebering together through beautiful drawings.

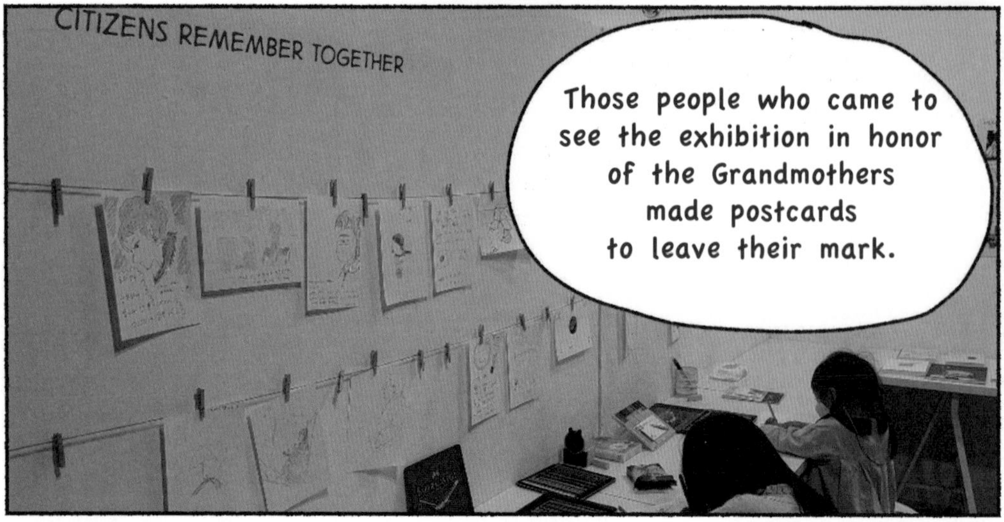
CITIZENS REMEMBER TOGETHER
Those people who came to see the exhibition in honor of the Grandmothers made postcards to leave their mark.

* The Remembering Together Project Grandmothers, Our Grandmothers exhibition, Seoul Community College, Red Brick Gallery, from Sept. 12, 2020 to Dec. 21st, 2020. Hosted by Seoul City, Organized by The Picture Book Art Citizen Group.

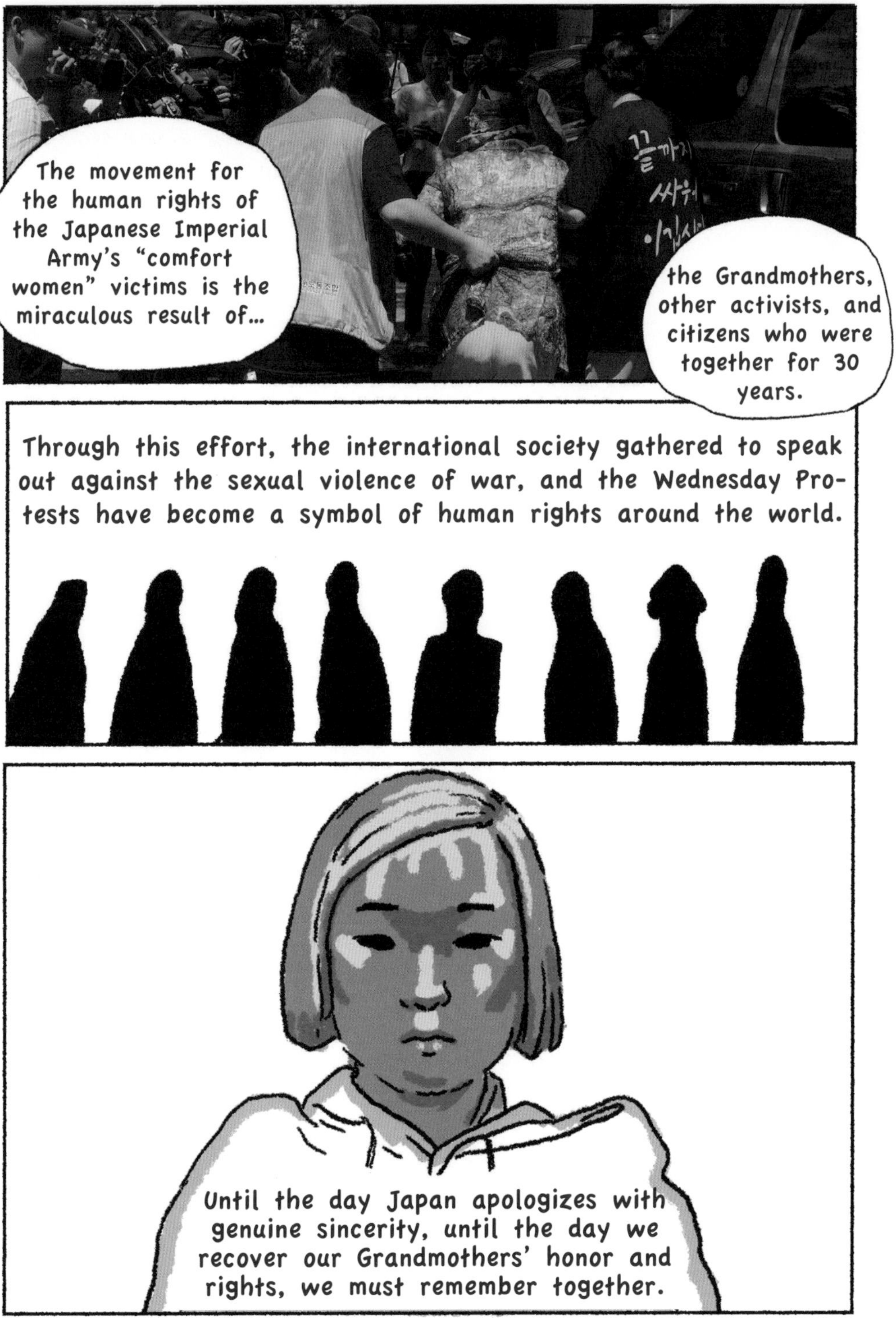
The movement for the human rights of the Japanese Imperial Army's "comfort women" victims is the miraculous result of...
the Grandmothers, other activists, and citizens who were together for 30 years.
Through this effort, the international society gathered to speak out against the sexual violence of war, and the Wednesday Protests have become a symbol of human rights around the world.
Until the day Japan apologizes with genuine sincerity, until the day we recover our Grandmothers' honor and rights, we must remember together.

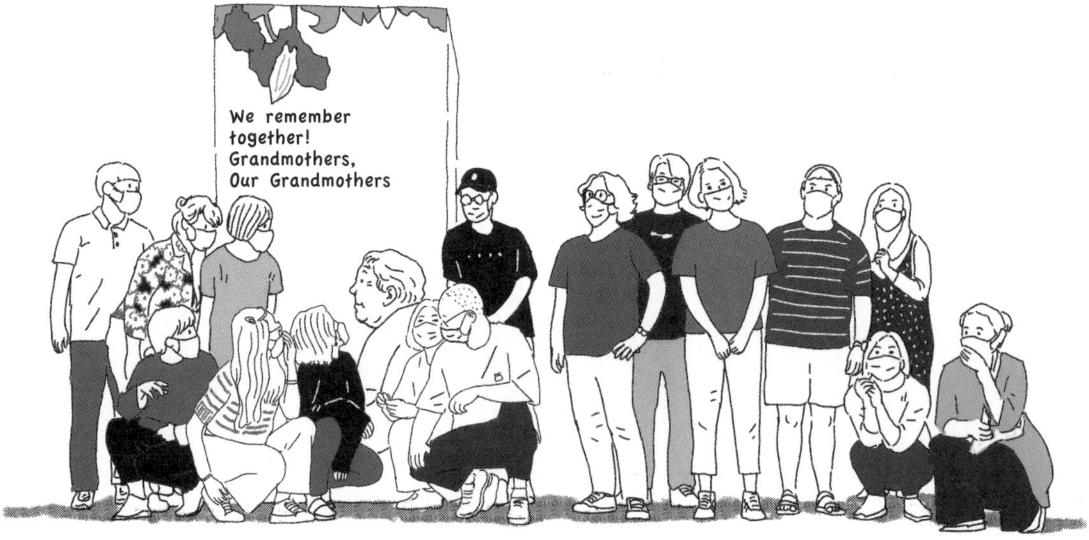
We remember
together!
Grandmothers,
Our Grandmothers

We will not forget you.
What is remembered will last forever.

Resources

There are many websites and online videos that share history, testimony, and the public's response to this very important human rights issue. Here are just a few to explore.

"Comfort Women": the Unresolved History (https://remembercomfortwomen.org/history-background/comfort-women-the-unresolved-history/)

"Comfort Women" Justice Coalition (https://remembercomfortwomen.org/)

Digital Museum: The Comfort Women Issue and he Asian Women's Fund (https://www.awf.or.jp/e1/index.html)

Education for Social Justice Foundation (http://www.e4sjf.org/primary-source-documents-comfort-women-history-and-issues.html)

A Guide to Understanding the History of the 'Comfort Women' Issue. United States Institute of Peace (https://www.usip.org/publications/2022/09/guide-understanding-history-comfort-women-issue)

Project Sonyeo (https://www.projectsonyeo.com/)

The Story of Japan's "Comfort Women" (https://sofrep.com/news/the-story-of-japans-comfort-women/)

Who are the "Comfort Women"? (comfort-women.org)

World War II Japan's "Comfort Women" And The Horrific Sexual Slavery They Endured (https://allthatsinteresting.com/comfort-women)

Video:

Behind the Story: the Legacy of Comfort Women

https://www.youtube.com/watch?v=EpRRn7gemdI

Former "Comfort Woman" Recalls Horrors

(https://video.search.yahoo.com/yhs/search?fr=yhs-ima-st_mig&ei=UTF-8&hsimp=yhs-st_mig&hspart=ima&p=comfort+women+testimony&type=q3000_A07ZH_ext_bcrq#id=1&vid=2fd6816dae49b8ea86895f311d4a0636&action=click)

History of the Comfort Women—the Apology |POV| PBS (https://www.youtube.com/watch?v=qsT97ax_Xb0)

In the Name of the Emperor - Comfort Women Segment

https://www.youtube.com/watch?v=vK3a4qz3srQ

Jan Ruff-O'Herne Tells Her Horrible Ordeal As WW2 Comfort Woman

https://www.dailymail.co.uk/news/article-3450302/Jan-Ruff-O-Herne-93-forced-comfort-woman-WWII-pursuing-Japanese-government-damages.html

Life As A "Comfort Woman": Story of Kim Bok-Dong (https://www.youtube.com/watch?v=qsT97ax_Xb0)

One Last Cry - 1. Introduction, Philippine Comfort Women Story (https://www.youtube.com/watch?v=ISMaMzLT4MM)

One Last Cry - 2. Comfort Women Story in China

(https://www.youtube.com/watch?v=gVq_C2OCspo)

Researchers Claim This Is The First Video Showing Korean "Comfort Women"

https://www.youtube.com/watch?v=3Sn1a3ZqO20

Note: A number of scholarly books and articles have been written on the "comfort women," so be sure to check your library and online book vendors, and keep surfing the internet to learn more about this and other human rights issues. Human rights violations affect everyone on this earth. We cannot afford to close our eyes or look away.

My sincere thanks to those who have helped me from start to finish in recording the stories of Grandmothers, Our Grandmothers.

—Han Seong-won

Published by Tuttle Publishing, an imprint of Periplus Editions (HK) Ltd.

www.tuttlepublishing.com

Published in Korea as:
할머니, 우리 할머니: 일본군 '위안부' 피해자 할머니를 기억합니다 by 한성원
Grandmothers, Our Grandmothers : We Remember Our Grandmothers, Who Were Forced To Be "Comfort Women" for the Japanese Imperial Army by Han, Seong-won
Copyright © 2020 by Han, Seong-won
This English language edition was published by Periplus Editions (HONG KONG) Ltd. in 2023 by arrangement with Sodong Publishing House through KCC (Korea Copyright Center Inc.), Seoul.
Translated from Korean by Soo Kyung Lee
Copyright © 2023 Periplus Edition (HK) Ltd.
ISBN 978-0-8048-5663-8

Library of Congress Cataloging-in-Publication Data is in process.

27 26 25 24 23   6 5 4 3 2 1

Printed in China   2303EP

Distributed by:

North America, Latin America and Europe
Tuttle Publishing, 364 Innovation Drive, North Clarendon, VT 05759-9436.
Tel: 1 (802) 773 8930; Fax: 1 (802) 773 6993
info@tuttlepublishing.com
www.tuttlepublishing.com

Asia Pacific
Berkeley Books Pte Ltd
3 Kallang Sector #04-01,
#02-12 Singapore 349278.
Tel: (65) 6741 2178; Fax: (65) 6741 2179
inquiries@periplus.com.sg
www.tuttlepublishing.com

TUTTLE PUBLISHING® is a registered trademark of Tuttle Publishing, a division of Periplus Editions (HK) Ltd.

"Books to Span the East and West"

Tuttle Publishing was founded in 1832 in the small New England town of Rutland, Vermont [USA]. Our core values remain as strong today as they were then—to publish best-in-class books which bring people together one page at a time. In 1948, we established a publishing outpost in Japan—and Tuttle is now a leader in publishing English-language books about the arts, languages and cultures of Asia. The world has become a much smaller place today and Asia's economic and cultural influence has grown. Yet the need for meaningful dialogue and information about this diverse region has never been greater. Over the past seven decades, Tuttle has published thousands of books on subjects ranging from martial arts and paper crafts to language learning and literature—and our talented authors, illustrators, designers and photographers have won many prestigious awards. We welcome you to explore the wealth of information available on Asia at **www.tuttlepublishing.com**.